# ECONOMIC CONVERSATIONS

## THE SIMPLE SIDE OF A COMPLEX SUBJECT

DRISHTI VERMA

Made with ♥ on the Notion Press Platform
www.notionpress.com

To my parents and my brother—

Thank you for believing in me,
for encouraging me to write,
and for always being my biggest support.
This book is dedicated to the three of you.

# Contents

# Disclaimer

This book contains original illustrations and analogies inspired by fictional scenes from popular Indian films. These references are used solely for educational, illustrative, and transformative purposes to explain economic concepts in an accessible and relatable manner.

All characters, settings, and film names mentioned or referred to are the property of their respective copyright holders.

No copyright infringement is intended.

This book is not affiliated with, authorized by, or endorsed by any film production house or copyright owner.

# Preface

I didn't write this book to teach economics.
I wrote it to remind you that you're already living it.

Everything around us—what we buy, what we skip, why prices rise, why salaries don't keep up, why some people have more while others struggle—is all economics. It's not just a subject in a classroom. It's the background music of our daily lives. And yet, most of us grow up never really seeing it that way.

I remember the first time I studied economics—in 11$^{th}$ standard. It felt like I had discovered a language that explained the world. But the more I read, the more I thought, Why didn't I learn this earlier? If I had started understanding economics in 5$^{th}$ or 6$^{th}$ grade, I would've seen money, markets, and even human behavior so differently.

That thought stayed with me.
And eventually, it became this book.

I wrote *Economic Conversations* so that no one has to wait until they're older—or more "qualified"—to understand the system they're already a part of. I wanted to write the kind of book I wish I had—something that didn't feel like a textbook, didn't scare you with graphs or jargon, and didn't make economics feel distant or difficult.

This book is for the curious 10-year-old, the confused college student, the working professional who never liked numbers, and the everyday person who just wants to make sense of how things work. My only goal is this: to make economics feel less like a subject and more like a conversation—one that anyone can join.

If this book makes you think, question, smile, or simply feel less intimidated by the word economics, then it's done its job.

— Drishti

# Introduction

Let me ask you something: when you hear the word economics, what comes to mind? Complicated graphs? Fancy terms? Maybe a bit of yawning? You're not alone. For years, economics has been treated like a subject meant only for experts in suits or professors with whiteboards full of equations. But the truth is—economics is for everyone.

We all make economic decisions every single day. From choosing between two food items at the grocery store to deciding whether to spend or save, we are all, knowingly or unknowingly, participating in an economic system. Yet, so many of us feel like we "don't get it."

That's exactly why I wrote this book.

*Economic Conversations* is my humble attempt to take economics out of classrooms and boardrooms and bring it to your living room couch or your chai break at work. Through stories, everyday examples, and even a sprinkle of Bollywood references, I want to show you that economics isn't scary. It's actually quite intuitive—once you strip away the jargon.

This book doesn't assume you have any background in economics. In fact, I've written it in such a way that even a fifth-grader could read it and feel confident talking about opportunity cost, inflation, or the basics of banking.

Each chapter is designed like a conversation—a relaxed back-and-forth that you'd have with a curious friend. My goal isn't to teach you textbook definitions. It's to help you feel the ideas, relate them to real life, and maybe even enjoy learning economics for the first time.

So grab your favorite snack or a cup of chai, and let's chat. I promise, by the end of this book, you won't just understand economics—you might even start to like it.

### CHAPTER ONE

# FUNDAMENTALS: SCARCITY, OPPORTUNITY COST AND TRADE-OFFS

## *Resources: The Basis of Every Human Need*

Before we delve into this chapter, here's a task for you! Look around yourself. Can you spot any item made from wood? Maybe a piece of furniture! Who would have made it? How much money would have been invested to get the right equipment and machinery to make an excellent finish? Now, can you think of a furniture brand? Do you know who the founder/owner of that brand is? Well, you might have an answer, but these questions are not to test your General Knowledge. These are your entry passes to the world of economics!

The various inputs used to produce goods and services are referred to as Resources in economics. The wood from which the furniture is made is part of the natural resources, which come from what we refer to in economics as the Land. The carpenters who designed and carved out a beautiful piece of furniture form the Labour, or

Human Resources. The tools, machinery, and factories set up to complete the task are part of the Capital Resources. The owners of the furniture brand who put their minds and skills to bring everything together through innovation and management are part of Entrepreneurship.

All goods and services are produced to satisfy human needs and wants, which are unlimited, by the way! On the contrary, the resources, as we discussed above, are limited in supply. The whole foundation of economics is laid on this concept: Scarcity of Resources. We cannot have everything we want and desire. So, what do we do? Make choices!

If you have seen the movie *Yeh Jawani Hai Deewani*, you would remember a dialogue exchanged between the two protagonists when they were exploring a city. Deepika Padukone's character (*Naina*) was nothing but talking about opportunity cost. In the scene, they had two plans at hand. Ranbir Kapoor's character (*Bunny*) wanted to go and see a light show, while Naina wanted to enjoy the sunset. Since both events were happening at the same time, they had to choose between the two. The choice was made because of the scarcity of resources - here, time! Naina chose sunset over the other option, and that was her opportunity cost - missing the light show. So, in technical terms, opportunity cost refers to the value of the next best alternative forgone when a decision is made. Well, you might think that such dilemmas happen once in a while. We can enjoy everything. It's all about management. But that is not true. All resources are limited, and since they are limited, we need to choose where to put that resource to use, for the best possible outcome.

To think of an example, let's say you (in your teenage years) went to a market to buy a pair of shoes for yourself. You only have      ₹2000 as your pocket money. When you went to the market, you found the exact shoes you wanted in a shop. But just beside the shop, you saw a very cool sweatshirt at the same price as your shoes. Since you only have limited pocket money and your parents won't give you more money, you have to decide between the two. You thought that you already had one pair of shoes, but since winter is approaching,, you thought that you would need a cozy sweatshirt to keep you warm. Therefore, instead of buying shoes, you went for the sweatshirt. Here, the opportunity cost is the shoes you gave up. Although the prices of both items were the same, you had to choose because you had limited resources - here, money. But hey! There's even more to this story, which we will come back to in a bit. Let us first see why opportunity cost holds so much power in the world of economics.

## Costs and Trade-Offs: Choices in Governance

Whenever we talk about resources and their allocation, the most common thing that comes to our mind is: Budget. Every year, before the start of the financial year, a year-long budget is prepared and presented in the Parliament and State Legislative Assemblies, in which the government of the day estimates its revenue and how and where it will spend that money. If you have ever looked at the budget document, you must have seen the sector-wise or ministry-wise distribution of government funds. The government has limited resources with itself. In most cases, the revenue from taxes is not sufficient to meet the needs of the people, so they opt to borrow, both from the domestic market and the global market. Now, they have to decide what to do with the capital raised. How to best utilize them since they are to be paid back with interest. You must be aware of the debate on freebies in recent times. It's about government expenditure on subsidies, and free distributions of goods and services - like food grains, electricity, bicycles, etc. The funds used to provide such freebies can be used elsewhere. When the government decides to allocate funds to one project, say, highway construction, there is an opportunity cost attached to it. The same funds could have been used to construct schools in remote areas or buy defense equipment to protect the border regions.

If we take a look at the Indian budget for FY 2023-24[1], ₹5.94 lakh crore was allocated to defence, ₹1.6 to rural development, and ₹ 1.13 lakh crore to education. In FY 2024-25[2], the defence sector got ₹4.54 lakh crores of funds, rural development got ₹2.65 lakh crores, and education got ₹1.25 lakh crores. These are just a few of the domains to do a comparative analysis. These three sectors got this much funding out of the total expenditure of ₹45 lakh crore in FY 2023-24. In the next year, when the total expenditure of the union government was ₹48 lakh crore, defence expenditure saw a decline, while rural development and education saw an uptick in fund allocation, compared to the previous financial year. The whole point of discussing these nuances of the budget is to make you understand how opportunity cost plays its role in governance and policy formulation.

To summarise what we have read till now, can we say that

opportunity costs are just about "where to put our money?" The answer is no! Let us again go back to the example of shoes versus the sweatshirt. We now know that since you had limited resources, i.e., money, you preferred a sweatshirt, and so, your opportunity cost was the shoes. But if we go one step further, it's not the shoes but the values held with the shoes that are your opportunity cost. You chose the values like warmth, comfort, and style that the sweatshirt would bring to you, while forgoing the value of, say, ease of walking, flexing the shoe brand among your peer group. The cost in opportunity cost can be anything - monetary aspect, social aspect, emotional aspect, or functional aspect. The list is non-exhaustive.

## Public Policy and Opportunity Cost: A Deep Dive

As we discussed in the previous section, every decision made is nothing but a choice among the various alternatives we have. Choosing one means leaving the other options, and the value held with those options is our opportunity cost. Decisions made by any government have an impact on millions of people. We elect the government and give them the power to choose for us. So, how does the government decide which options to let go of and which ones to implement? There are principles and theories under public policy that talk about this. Let us explore some of them, with opportunity cost at the center of our discussion.

One of the most prominent theories regarding the decision-making process is the Rational Choice Theory. It assumes that choices are made by comparing the costs and benefits of various alternatives and choosing those that provide the maximum benefits or utility.

This theory accounts for opportunity costs to ensure that resources are allocated where they provide the greatest benefit. For example, the introduction of Direct Benefits Transfer (DBT). The administrative cost involved in implementing the DBT could have been used elsewhere, but the benefits of DBT seemed much wider, covering so many citizens receiving benefits in the form of direct transfers or subsidies. This would also ensure that there are no leaks in such a transfer, plus, in the long run, the cost of transfer would be reduced due to resource optimization. However, this theory is based on the assumption of greatest utility, which is not always the case in decision-making.

According to another theory, called Public Choice theory, choices are made based on the self-interest of the decision-makers. The trade-offs involved in resource allocation are based on the interests of the decision-makers, and that might not always be rational or optimal. For example, the scheme of free ration distribution. The resources deployed for its implementation could have been used to improve the skill level of the workforce. Such choices often reflect the interests of politicians to provide immediate relief to certain sections of society and thus, strengthen their voter base. However, the opportunity cost here is the potential growth of people who would have gained skills through vocational training that would have improved their employability in the long term.

Opportunity cost can also be linked to an interesting concept under public policy: Kaldor-Hicks Efficiency. This theory requires assessing if the gains from the chosen options are large enough to compensate for the losses, and thus, requires the decision-makers to account for the opportunity costs of the options they choose. For example, project approval for dam construction requires the displacement of people, deforestation, or loss of agricultural land. The resources used to construct the dam could be allocated to other areas, like solar energy projects. Under the Kaldor-Hicks theory, the dam will be considered efficient if the benefits gained from dam construction outweigh the opportunity costs. This theory is an improvement over the Pareto efficiency since it includes compensating for the loss incurred while going for one alternative. Pareto efficiency refers to the allocation of resources in a way that makes someone better off, by making someone else lose something. It's like either of the two parties involved can be the beneficiary when reallocating resources. Knowing the opportunity costs, thus, helps in assessing what is being sacrificed and ensuring that the trade-offs are justified.

## Opportunity Cost at the International Level

David Ricardo's concept of comparative advantage, in which he explains why a country should specialise in producing certain goods and engage in trade in other goods, can be linked to the the concept of opportunity costs[3]. Let's take a simple example involving two countries: India and the USA. Taking all resources into consideration, hypothetically assume that the two countries can only produce two goods - Chocolates and Chips (taking simple goods for easy comprehension). Let's say India can produce 100 chocolate bars or 500 packets of Chips in a day, while the USA can produce 200 Chocolate bars or 400 packets of chips in a day. This means that for India, at the cost of producing 1 chocolate bar, it can alternatively produce 5 packets of chips, whereas, for the USA, at the cost of producing 1 chocolate bar, it can only produce 2 packets of chips. Thus, the USA has a comparative advantage in chocolate production while India has a comparative advantage in chips production. According to this theory, India should specialise in chips production and import chocolates and vice versa for the USA. By specializing in goods with lower opportunity costs, both countries can trade and gain. This leads to a more efficient resource allocation globally, increasing the overall output and welfare.

However, this theory has been criticized because overspecialisation may lead to increased risks from the vulnerability in external markets. Countries in the Middle East whose economies are highly dependent on oil exports are now looking for diversification for this reason.

We saw how so many theories in policy-making involve the application of opportunity cost. Remember that where there is a decision, there is an opportunity cost.

## Business, Profits, and Opportunity Costs

After meandering through the arena of public policy, let us now shift our focus to the organizational level. Just like the government has limited resources for ensuring the welfare of its people, businesses, too, have limited resources within which they have to achieve their goals and targets. The application of opportunity cost in business covers diverse areas, including resource allocation, budget management, strategic decision-making, profit maximization, and risk assessment. Where should the company make investments, which marketing channels to opt for, how much time to devote to a project, which product category to invest more in, how much profit to keep as reserves, and how much to give as dividends to the shareholders, when to go for an IPO (Initial Public Offering), which areas to outsource and which ones to keep in-house, which celebrity to hire as the brand ambassador, and even what should the work culture be like - hierarchical or inclusive, what should be the design of the office space - cubicle, open, or virtual, from major to minor decisions, all involves opportunity cost that companies need to assess. Only such companies sustain in the long run that carefully consider all opportunity costs - explicit and implicit, in their decision-making process.

Explicit opportunity cost can be the various alternatives that could have been done instead of the chosen option. What about the implicit opportunity costs? Various values are hidden or are very indirect in nature. In economics, there's a concept of externality. It refers to the costs or benefits that arise from any economic activity that affects those not directly involved, for example, the decision of a company or government to set up mines for exploring critical minerals. The alternatives forgone could be any other economic activity. Such alternatives are explicit in nature. However, in the process of exploration, there could be destruction of a whole ecosystem thriving there. The loss of carbon sinks due to deforestation is an example of a negative externality. Externalities often represent the social and environmental opportunity costs that are often neglected. Global warming and climate change are the biggest examples of negative externalities. The concept of Externality is discussed in the 6th chapter in greater detail.

A CEO of a social media company sitting in Silicon Valley would take into consideration the alternatives forgone while developing its algorithm, but would they consider the social cost of deteriorating mental health of young people? Choosing not to address externalities also involves opportunity costs. For example, many social media platforms are pushing for more and more content creation and views to attract advertisements from companies. However, in this process, the productivity level of the masses might go down, and in the long run, there could arise a situation where people lack the skills required to get a job. With the rise in unemployment, advertisements through social media channels would then become unprofitable for the companies, since the purchasing power would automatically go down. This, in turn, could ultimately backfire on those social media platforms that are, today, pushing for all sorts of unproductive viewership. Thus, it becomes important for companies to take into consideration even the social costs involved to sustain themselves in the long run.

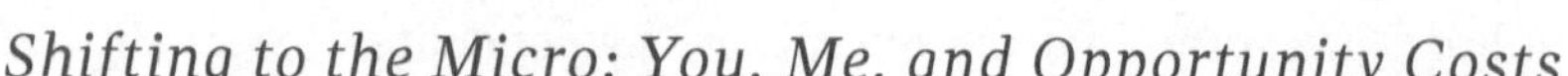

## Shifting to the Micro: You, Me, and Opportunity Costs

We talked about the government and businesses. Now, let us come down to the basic unit: You and me. Resource allocation is not just limited to the macro level. Decisions are made by everyone, and as mentioned earlier, where there is a decision, there is an opportunity cost. According to various surveys, on average, an adult makes 33,000-35,000 decisions in a day[4]. When we are making so many decisions on a daily basis, shouldn't we be thinking about the opportunity costs involved with them? If you recall, we started this chapter with an example involving us: shoes vs the sweatshirt. Similar to this, we assess various alternatives before doing every task. The opportunity cost of you reading this book now could be the time spent on social media or a chat with your friend. If you are a student right now, what could be your opportunity cost? Maybe a job that you didn't take up because you preferred higher education over immediate income.

## The Economics of Attention

If you think you don't have access to too many resources, to pay attention to opportunity cost, because you feel you have still under-achieved in your career, or you are still a student who hasn't started earning yet, you need to cheer up a little today. This is because you have the most important resource that the industries are fighting for: Attention. Humans have finite attention, and so, it can be directed towards one activity, thought, or person at a time. Every time we choose to do a task, it's the allocation of our attention.

Since we have limited attention, the opportunity cost of our attention is the potential experience we sacrifice when we focus our mental energy on any particular activity. Brands and advertisers are spending millions of bucks just to grab our attention. For us, the 5 seconds ad before clicking on the skip button is just a regular thing, but for the advertisers, those 5 seconds are so important that a whole team of brand strategists and experts work together to decide what to show in those first 5 seconds to leave their imprint and force the viewers to stay a little more before skipping. If you are reading this right now, I, as an author, have succeeded in buying your attention when you could have allocated your focus to some other task at hand. Think of attention as a currency. Just like money, attention can be spent on anything. The value we get from it depends on the choices we make. So, the next time you scroll your social media, don't think it is free of cost. You are allocating your most precious resource to it, which could have been allocated to some other task where the return could have been much better.

## Getting into The Human Mind

Do we really think about the opportunity costs involved in each of our decisions? If we keep assessing all the costs and benefits of each choice, wouldn't that lead to decision paralysis? Opportunity costs are subjective in nature. It is different for everyone. This is because alternatives cannot always be quantified in monetary terms. The values we assign to experiences are different for different people. For someone who feels deprived of emotional bonding would prioritise spending their resources - time, money, or energy - on their social relationships. For them, giving up on a high-paying job in a prime city wouldn't be difficult because they want to stay with their family in their hometown. Some people say they want to have it all. But from the angle of economics, it is practically impossible to have it all. There are always trade-offs we make. The inability to choose various alternative paths can be tied to the concept of 'regret'. Regret is the emotional counterpart to the logical concept of opportunity cost. While opportunity cost provides a framework for evaluating our decisions, regret reminds us of the emotional side of those evaluations. For example, buying an expensive car might generate a feeling of regret later if an unexpected expense arises, as the opportunity cost of buying the car was the financial security forgone.

Although we can't achieve everything we want, we can still achieve 'many' things. This is where delegation and automation come to our rescue. We need to learn to prioritize the tasks at hand, delegate those that can be outsourced, and automate those where technology can help. This will make our lives less chaotic and more successful. Think about some major trade-offs you have made so far, and their opportunity costs.

If we talk about the macro-level, the best ways to deal with resource scarcity are: Innovation and technological advancements. For example, the invention of fuel-efficient engines has reduced the per-unit consumption of fuels like coal and fossil fuels. However, there's an interesting concept called Jevons Paradox, proposed by economist William Stanley Jevons, which states that an increase in the efficiency of a resource, paradoxically, increases its consumption instead of a decline. Although the per-unit consumption would reduce, the overall consumption at the macro-level would increase because of higher demand. Better efficiency brings down the price per unit of resources, which, in turn, allows more people to afford them. This is referred to as the Rebound Effect. So, does that mean innovations and technological advancements are worthless? No, not at all. Jevons Paradox aims to make us realise that improving efficiency is not a silver bullet to resolve resource scarcity. Innovations still matter. Due to innovations, there is access to better alternatives and substitutes.

For instance, the emergence of renewable energy as an alternative source of power, use of synthetic materials as an alternative to natural materials. Innovations and improved efficiencies need to be paired with smart policies and behavioural shifts. We need to promote a sustainable lifestyle where we use resources in a way that doesn't put our future generation at stake. The government needs to promote the circular economy in which we follow the 3R principle: Reduce, Reuse, and Recycle. This ensures that the resources get back into the cycle again instead of a one-time utilisation. Our brief discussion on demand and price, in this section, sets the stage for the next chapter, where we talk about what is often referred to as the market forces in economics. Find out what!

[1] Ministry of Finance. (2023). *Union Budget 2023-24.* Government of India.

[2] Ministry of Finance. (2024). *Union Budget 2024-25.* Government of India.

[3] Krugman, P. R., & Obstfeld, M. (2018). *International economics: Theory and policy* (11th ed.). Pearson.

[4] Milkman, K. L. (2023, December). A simple way to make better decisions. *Harvard Business Review*

# THE MARKET FORCES: DEMAND AND SUPPLY

Just a few days before starting to write this chapter, I went to buy groceries from the market. Winters had just started. The total bill was ₹240. Out of this, 1 kilogram of Papaya cost me ₹40. When I went to the shop next week, its price had dropped to ₹10 per kg. What happened in 7 days that led to a 75% decline in its price? The answer lies in the interplay of the concepts of demand and supply. We will come back to this part in later sections.

In the evergreen movie *Sholay*, there a very famous said by the main antagonist of the movie (played by Amjad Khan), asking his men how many people were present in the village, in a particular scene. In the movie, the two main protagonists - played by Dharmendra and Amitabh Bachchan - were considered the heroes by the village people. This was because the villagers needed protection from the antagonist, and they were unable to fight on their own. We need to see this situation in the movie as an interesting example of what we are going to talk about in this chapter - demand and supply. The demand, here, was for people who could fight with the antagonist, but the supply of such people was less, only two. This mismatch in demand and supply of fighters increased the value of the two protagonists, and therefore, they were the heroes.

## Basics of Demand and Supply

In economics, demand can be defined as the willingness and ability of consumers to buy goods or services at a specific price within a particular period of time. According to the law of demand, there is an inverse relationship between the price and demand for goods or services. Keeping other factors constant, when the price of a commodity drops, its demand rises, whereas if the price increases, the demand drops. Why would we buy something at an expensive price? But if the shopkeeper gives us a discount, wouldn't we be attracted to buy them? This law is based on the assumption that consumers behave rationally, where they want to maximize their utility by purchasing more at lower prices. In the previous chapter on opportunity cost, we discussed the premise of utility maximization in brief, under the section of rational choice theory. We will discuss more on this in later sections. For now, just understand that utility, in economics, refers to the benefits or satisfaction we derive from consuming a good or service.

Supply refers to the willingness and ability of the producer to provide goods or services at a specific price to the consumer. The law of supply states that, keeping all other factors constant, an increase/decrease in the price of any product increases/decreases its supply in the market. Thus, there is a direct relationship between the price and supply of a commodity. For example, if the price of video game consoles is rising, manufacturers of gaming consoles would ramp up their supply. This is because, at higher prices, the producers would earn higher profits. Even the law of supply is based on the assumption that producers are driven by their desire to maximize their profits. Now that we have a basic idea of how the demand and supply of goods and services react to their prices, let's dive deeper into the hows and whys of it.

## Some Logic and Insights

We now know that cheaper things are more in demand and expensive ones less. But here's a reverse question: what happens to the price if the demand is high? Will there still be an inverse relationship between the two? No. We need to understand that the two situations are not the same. In the first one, price changes are the cause and change in demand is the effect, while in the second situation, the change in demand is the cause, and price change is the effect. The law of demand, basically, talks about how consumers react to price changes. Similarly, the law of supply talks about how producers react to changes in prices. Price changes as an effect are discussed in the 3$^{th}$ chapter in greater detail.

Keeping price changes as the cause, let us understand the logic behind the way demand and supply react to it. We already know the basic assumptions behind both the laws - utility maximization for consumers and profit maximization for producers, respectively. But there's more to it. Here's a scenario - you went to buy your all-time favourite chocolate bar, but due to certain factors, the price has doubled. What you got at ₹50 now costs you ₹100. What will you do in such a situation? Return home empty-handed? What about your intense cravings? You saw the chocolate counter and searched for some other options within your budget. Thus, you could fulfill your satisfaction at the same price. This is what we call the substitution effect. You had other options, and so, neither did you sacrifice your craving nor shed extra money from your pocket. No changes on your side, but the changes that took place were on the side of that ₹100 chocolate bar. Its demand got reduced. Now let's take another situation where the price drops from ₹50 to ₹25. You went to buy one chocolate bar, but seeing the cheaper price, you decided to go for two bars. This is because the price drop has increased your purchasing capacity. This refers to the income effect. So, apart from utility maximization, other factors like substitution effect and income effect also provide the logic behind the inverse relation between demand and price.

Now let's turn to the producer side. Suppose the ₹50 chocolate bars are in great demand, so the producers decided to produce more and more of them. But to fulfill their production target, they had to expand their factory size, they imported expensive machinery for large-scale production. This led to increased production costs. Thus, to remain profitable, they decided to increase the market price of their chocolates so that they could recover their investments. Therefore, changes in the cost of production, full capacity utilization of its production units, and to remain profitable, the producers adjust the final prices of goods or services accordingly.

There's a very interesting concept in economics that lays the foundation for demand and supply - Marginal Utility. We know what utility is. But what is marginal utility, and how is it related to the law of supply and demand? Marginal utility refers to the additional utility or satisfaction we get from consuming one more unit of a good or service. Imagine you were craving your favourite pizza! So you went to your favorite restaurant and placed an order for it. You started eating the first slice, and felt like heaven! As you ate your pizza, with every slice, your craving lowered a bit. By the time you ate that last slice of pizza, you were almost satisfied and felt full. Then, a waiter came and asked for any other orders. You said no and were about to leave, but then, you saw an offer on the menu that said 40% discount on your second order. This made you feel excited, and you went for another round. Why did you order another pizza when you were almost satisfied with one? This is the theory of diminishing marginal utility and how it forms the basis for the inverse relation between price and demand. With every slice of pizza, the utility or satisfaction you gained got reduced. The utility from the last slice was way lower than the utility from the first one. Since you were getting lower utility, you didn't want to buy another pizza. But as soon as you saw the discount offer, the low utility got compensated with the lower price. You became willing to pay a lower price for the next pizza.

You must have observed various offers like subscriptions to OTT platforms, or mobile data packs where you are required to pay more for regular models like monthly ones, but less for additional/ booster packs like add-ons. This is because of the law of diminishing marginal utility, where we are willing to pay less for additional units of a good or service.

## *Deviations in the Law*

The basic principles underlying demand and supply are discussed. Now, it's time to let the rebels come out of the box. Some goods and services act like rebels and are defiant. They don't conform to the law of demand. The first category is called Giffen goods. These are some low-quality, inferior goods whose price, despite being on the rise, has higher demand in the market. People below the poverty line, who cannot afford better alternatives, would continue to buy inferior products because of their lower purchasing power. The income effect, discussed in an earlier section, overpowers the substitution effect. For example, coarse grains. Then there are goods called Veblen goods, which are in high demand because they are priced higher. All those branded shoes, bags, watches, or luxury cars are bought because they are expensive. The logic behind this is the social status and brand value associated with these products. If the owners of a luxury car brand lowered their prices to make it less premium, their cars would lose their brand value, and people would switch to other, more premium alternatives. Apart from the inferior and superior quality products/services, there are certain basic necessity goods/services that are always in demand irrespective of their price. For example, life-saving medicines. Such goods are inelastic. We will discuss this concept very soon.

Coming to the law of supply, there are categories of goods/services that do not conform to the law of supply. In other words, their supply does not depend on the price changes. Some goods have a fixed supply, like a stadium. The seating capacity would not change even when the price of tickets fluctuates. Then there are perishable goods whose shelf life is much shorter, like fruits. Sellers would sell such goods even at lower prices near their expiration, to avoid spoilage, regardless of their prevailing market price. Even Veblen goods like limited edition luxury watches. Their supply is restricted to ensure their exclusivity, despite price rises. In the labour market, certain types of professions don't follow the general law of supply. Despite getting higher wages, the working hours (supply) are fewer. For example, professionals like doctors, despite getting high payments, might prefer to work for fewer hours to ensure sufficient breaks between surgeries, or just to have a work-life balance. This, in technical language, is referred to as the Backward-Bending Supply Curve. Other factors for restricted supply could be government intervention, like export quotas, defence manufacturing rights, and exceptional situations like natural disasters or labour strikes.

## When Demand Meets Supply: Understanding Market Equilibrium

The price at which we buy anything is the equilibrium price. At this price, the quantity in demand matches the quantity supplied. As soon as any one of the two exceeds the other, the equilibrium gets disturbed. Take a sheet of paper and draw two lines intersecting each other, similar to what looks like the alphabet "X". The two lines depict the demand and supply curves, and the point of intersection is the market equilibrium. Remember the Papaya example we discussed at the start of this chapter? It's time to reveal the reason behind the 75% decline in its cost within a week. As I mentioned, winter had just started when the price was ₹40. Within a week, the temperatures went down drastically, and so did the diet of people. Papaya is often avoided in winter. As the demand for papaya in the market declined, the quantity supplied exceeded the quantity demanded. This demand-supply mismatch disturbed the state of market equilibrium. Thus, the sellers reduced the prices. When prices went down from ₹40 to ₹10 per kg, demand for Papaya boosted. As demand rose, it matched the quantity supplied, thus regaining the equilibrium. For starters, it must be noted that the prices did not drop directly from ₹40 to ₹10. The decline happened gradually. It would be possible for the price to go further down to, say, ₹5 per kg if the demand did not match the level of supply at ₹ 10.

Now, when you go to the grocery market on random days and observe price changes, you know that either the demand or the supply of the commodity is fluctuating, causing a shift in its price levels. The best example for price adjustments to maintain market equilibrium is the cab booking applications, where price changes every few minutes to adjust to the demand and supply of cars. But what about those items whose prices haven't been changed for a long time? They have a stable market. Do you know any such item?

## The Rubber Band Effect: Concept of Price Elasticity

Let's go back to the chocolate bar example, where you bought a different brand of chocolate because the price of your favourite one had gone up. How easy was it for you to switch to an alternate option? For most of us, it would be an easy decision, given that we have a similar level of trust in the other brand. But there are times when we go to the shop to buy something for ourselves, and they are out of stock. In such times, we return empty-handed. Why don't we buy alternatives? Maybe because we trust only the brand that we were looking for. In the former case, a slight change in the price can make us switch to alternatives, while in the latter case, even when we know that the item has gone out of stock and new stock will come with a higher price tag, we are willing to wait but buy only that particular brand. The two situations aptly depict the concept of price elasticity of demand. It shows how easily the demand for a particular good or service changes in response to a change in its price. Diabetes is now a household thing in India. If you know people around you who are diabetic, you would know that they have to take insulin in the form of tablets/injections. Such medicines are inelastic because people will buy them irrespective of the price level. Lack of substitutes, monopoly, or high brand value are some of the factors for the inelasticity of goods or services.

Similarly, the price elasticity of supply refers to the responsiveness of the quantity supplied to changes in price. Certain goods, like agricultural produce, cannot be changed quickly in response to their changing prices. Such goods are inelastic. Knowing the elasticity of goods and services is very important. For producers, it helps in deciding the price of their products. Inelastic products are sold at high margins and thus help the producers gain more profits, while elastic goods have very competitive pricing to compete with their substitutes. It is helpful for the government as well. Inelastic goods like alcohol or cigarettes are generally taxed high, thus enhancing the state revenue. Remember the long queues at the liquor shops during lockdown? The taxes from liquor filled the state's purse. Think of price elasticity as someone who is very stubborn and someone who is very compliant. High elastic goods are the compliant ones, while inelastic goods are the stubborn ones. Find out which goods or services around you are elastic and which ones are inelastic.

To sum up, demand and supply are everywhere around us. Whenever you see price fluctuations, try to find out if the theory of supply and demand is at play, or if it's something else. If you observe closely, you'll notice that prices tend to rise more often than they fall. Why does this happen? Let's explore this in the next chapter.

### CHAPTER THREE

# COST OF LIVING: THE INFLATION PUZZLE

Picture this: It's 2014. Assume you were a kid at this point. You get ₹500 as your monthly pocket money from your parents. In about 3 years, you were able to save ₹10,000 after spending on different chores. You kept that money safe in your piggy bank, thinking you would use it sometime in the future. Over the years, you completely forgot about your piggy bank. Now, it's time to go to college. You have completed your school and are preparing to go to the hostel. While packing, you started clearing up your cupboard, and suddenly found your childhood piggy bank. On realizing you had saved ₹10,000, you got super excited. You could buy shoes of your favorite brand, for which your parents had said no! On opening the piggy bank, you found it had just ₹6000.

Surprised? You must be thinking, how come there was only ₹6000? Where did the rest of the money go? Did someone steal it? The answer is yes. Someone stole the money, and that "someone" is Inflation. We don't need to take this story in a literal sense. The piggy bank had exactly the same number of paper currencies and coins you would have kept. Here, we are talking about the value.

What was ₹10,000 in 2014 would not be the same in 2024. Let's understand the hows and whys of this topic.

If you have seen the movie *3 Idiots*, you would know how much the bhindi (Ladyfinger) costs. You would also know that soon, paneer would be sold at a jewellery shop. For context, there's a scene in the movie 3 Idiots where the mother of one of the characters is speaking to her son and his friends who had come to visit her. She talks about her struggles of managing everything - her husband's medicines, and her daughter's marriage. She complains about how expensive the vegetables are getting, especially the paneer, whose price has increased so much that soon, only rich people who could afford things like gold would buy it. In short, she's indirectly addressing the rising inflation. So, what exactly is inflation? By now, you would have gotten an idea of what we are talking about.

Inflation is the term used to describe a general rise in the prices of goods and services in the economy. Unlike what we discussed in the demand and supply chapter, where the price of a particular good or service rises due to higher demand or lower supply, inflation talks about a basket of goods and their prices at the macro level.

In the previous example of the piggy bank, the average inflation over the ten years is assumed to be 5%. Inflation means that what could be bought with those ₹10,000 ten years back would now be priced higher. Let's suppose we were able to buy 5 shirts for some amount ten years back, today, we would only be able to buy 3 shirts at the same price. We all must have heard such conversations from our parents and grandparents about how they used to get so many things with very little money. Here, the 5% inflation rate was an assumed number. So, how do we know the exact inflation rate? After all, there are so many goods and services in the market whose price keeps changing. For this, there are various instruments and indices that calculate the overall inflation in the economy over a period of time.

## Inflation Rate: How Do We Measure It?

In the Indian context, we have different indices like the Consumer Price Index (CPI), Wholesale Price Index (WPI), GDP Deflator, etc, that help us assess how much the prices of goods and services are rising at a general level. To get a more refined picture, there are many variants of such indices as well - CPI - Rural, CPI - Urban, CPI - Combined, CPI - Agricultural Labourers, CPI - Industrial Workers, etc. The basic method under all these indices is that they use a basket of goods and services that are assigned different weights, depending on their usage and importance. Then their average price is noted. Using a base year, changes in their price levels are monitored, with a final weighted average number. The changes are expressed in percentages. Without getting into the technical aspects of their methodology, let's say the overall prices of the whole basket of goods and services increased from ₹100 to ₹104 in one year. So, the inflation rate would be 4%. It's important to note that the base year is used as a reference point to calculate the index value. Inflation rates are generally calculated year-on-year, meaning comparing price levels of the present year with those of the previous year.

## CPI vs WPI: Who Says What?

What we see in the newspapers or news channels is the Headline Inflation. This inflation is nothing but CPI-Combined. India's central bank, the Reserve Bank of India, is entrusted with the task of controlling the inflation level in the economy. The RBI has a target range within which the inflation must be brought. The target range, presently (FY2024-25), the tolerable range of inflation, is 2%-6%. We will delve into how the RBI controls inflation in detail in a later section. For now, we must know that the rate being considered by the RBI is CPI-Combined. Why aren't they using WPI for inflation control? How is CPI different from WPI? Answers to these questions lie in the Index name itself. CPI covers the prices at the retail level - what you and I finally pay for a product, while WPI covers the prices at the wholesale level. Changes in the price of inputs or raw materials are better reflected in the WPI, while changes in the price of final goods and services are better reflected in the CPI. Another important factor for using CPI as headline inflation is that WPI does not consider price changes of services. Even the items included in the basket of both indices have different weightage. Inflation is a burn in our pockets. Higher inflation means we pay more than earlier. We, the final consumers, bear the brunt of inflation. Thus, the government working for our welfare needs to ensure that we are protected from very high inflation. For this, CPI gives a better picture.

Let us understand this with the help of an example. Suppose that the price of an important raw material - crude oil - has risen from $80/barrel to $100/barrel. Based on the weightage given to crude oil, the WPI would increase accordingly. For producers using crude oil as raw material, their cost of production would go high. Therefore, they would adjust the prices of their final product proportionately. However, let's say that the government provides a subsidy on that product. This means that the end consumer will have to pay a lower price due to the subsidy. Thus, despite a sharp rise in WPI, the CPI would show a nominal rise. Therefore, to better cater to the final consumers, the government and the RBI target to control the CPI. This, however, does not mean that WPI has no utility for policymakers. WPI holds significance as an early indicator of inflation. A rising WPI would mean that the CPI could also rise, thus helping the government early on. Producers and businesses also benefit from WPI, helping them adjust pricing strategies and manage profit margins. In other words, both WPI and CPI are complementary to each other, providing a broader picture of the price movements at different levels of the supply chain, thus helping in better price management.

## The Economics Behind Inflation

Here's a task for you: find the CPI and WPI rates of the Indian economy for the present, previous, and upcoming financial years. What trend do you see? Now, look at the inflation rate of Zimbabwe. You would observe a sharp difference in the level of inflation between the two economies. What factors play a role in inflation? The basic principle of price changes, as discussed in the previous chapter, is the mismatch between the demand and supply of goods or services. This principle finds its roots in the Keynesian theory of

Demand-Pull Inflation, where aggregate demand exceeds aggregate supply levels, thereby causing prices to rise. When people have more income at their disposal, they demand more. Say, if the government lowered the income tax for the salaried class. This would leave more money with the people, and now, they can buy more things for themselves. Thus, demand at the macro level, called aggregate demand, rises, pulling up the price. In such situations, to bring down the prices, the production level needs to be increased so that the supply matches the demand.

Economists like Milton Friedman, under the monetarist theory, believe that inflation is a monetary phenomenon. An excess of money supply in the economy leads to inflation. Think of it as too many hands chasing just a few goods. The excess of demand over supply is due to an artificial increase in money. The task of finding the inflation level of Zimbabwe was to substantiate this very point. One of the main reasons for such a high level of inflation in Zimbabwe was the printing of too many currencies by its central bank[1]. The denial of the demands for a stimulus package from the government for direct cash transfers to people during the COVID-19 lockdown was justified under this principle theory.

At times, there are constraints on the supply side. For instance, limited availability of raw material - supply chain disruptions like what happened during COVID-19 due to lockdown. Other reasons could be high cost of raw material pushing the price automatically, as discussed in the above crude oil example, other external shocks like natural disasters, a hike in wages, etc. In the present age of globalisation, when production has become so integrated and interdependent, supply-side constraints have become a huge risk. Certain sectors and companies in India are highly dependent on the raw materials from a particular economy. Such high dependence on one player is a risky job. The recent trend of diversification in supply chains is to reduce such dependence. Terms we often hear in the news, like China+1, Reshoring, Friendshoring, and De-risking, are all related to this domain. Inflation due to such supply-side constraints is referred to as Cost-Push Inflation.

There's also a theory called Structuralist Theory, under which inflation depends on structural factors within an economy. Structural factors, particularly, include the supply-side constraints. Other factors could include low productivity of industries, weak infrastructural ecosystem, and structural shifts from an agricultural-based economy to a service-based one can also contribute to inflation. If we take the case of India, food inflation is generally high due to low agricultural productivity and poor agri-market infrastructure. Logistics costs in India are also on the higher end, which contributes to higher prices.

In the era of technology and social media connectivity, the network effect is another factor that contributes to inflation. Network effect refers to a situation where the price of goods or services increases as more and more people use them. The underlying factor remains the same: demand-supply mismatch. For instance, with the rise in the user base on various social media platforms, the cost of advertising on such platforms has risen. Sometime back, Elon Musk had tweeted about some cryptocurrency. Soon after his tweet, the price of that currency skyrocketed due to the increased demand from traders[2]. This shows how the network effect causes inflation due to a large user base.

Expectations of future inflation, too, play a role in driving inflation. Let's suppose that people think that the prices of onions will rise in the near future. This induces them to start hoarding onions to protect their pockets. Such hoarding would create a demand-supply mismatch, thereby pushing up the prices. Sometimes, inflation expectations are not just limited to one commodity, but rather are general in nature. In such situations, workers often start demanding wage hikes to cope with higher living costs. Such demands, sometimes, even turn into strikes. The owners and management, to get going with the production, are compelled to hike their wages. This adds to the production costs, leading to higher prices for the end consumers. This can even turn into a vicious loop where a wage hike leads to a price hike and a price hike, in turn, leads to further demand for a wage hike. This phenomenon is called the Wage-Price Spiral.

## On The Other Side: Is Inflation Always Bad?

Looking at our discussions till now, it might seem that inflation is a problem. Well, it is! But beyond a certain level. Remember, we discussed that the RBI has a target range for inflation numbers: 2% to 6%. Why is it not targeting a 0% inflation rate? This is because moderate inflation is considered good for an economy. Let's see how! We know that there's something called investment - purchasing something that gives us some extra money along with the original value when sold after some time (called an asset). A very simple example of an investment is: Real Estate (Don't worry, we'll get to the complex examples as well in the 5th chapter!). Let's say, today you had ₹50 lakh with you and you decided to invest this money by purchasing a plot of land in your city. 5 years down the line, you decided to sell off the land. Here's a surprise! You were getting only ₹50 lakh, as per the existing market value of that land. You waited 5 years to get a hefty return from your investment, but alas, you couldn't. This is exactly what will happen if the inflation rate goes to 0%.

Inflation doesn't remain limited to your groceries and basic needs. It affects the value of all commodities. It is because of the expectations that the prices of certain items will go up, people choose to invest. If we get to know that the value of gold in the future will not rise, will we purchase gold jewellery? A business person may invest in machinery and equipment today, anticipating a higher price for their goods in the future. Moderate inflation encourages spending and investment. Inflation also benefits the borrowers. If you take a loan of, say, ₹1 lakh from a bank, which charges a fixed interest rate of 7%, and the current inflation rate is 4%, your real interest rate is 3% (7%-4%) only. This is because inflation has eroded the value of money. What is the value of money today will not be the same next year (lower purchasing power). To sum up, a moderate level of inflation should exist to ensure there's demand in the economy.

## Inflation and People: Finding Winners and Losers

Inflation doesn't affect everyone the same way[3]. There are two types of people: those who save money, just like keeping it in a piggy bank, and those who invest money. The former people often belong to the underserved, socially marginalised section of society. Many people still don't have access to basic financial services like a bank account. To ensure that inflation doesn't erode the value of our money, it's important to note that the return we are getting from any investment is higher than the prevailing rate of inflation. People working in the informal sector are mostly not covered under any social security benefits, which provide pension and insurance protection. Their wages are not regularly revised according to inflation. People with an awareness of inflation often invest in inflation-indexed financial instruments, meaning the returns are adjusted according to inflation. That is why you would see banks push up the interest rates on loans based on the prevailing inflation rates, to avoid making losses. Owners of tangible assets like gold, real estate, etc, are often at the winning end. This is because, during inflationary periods, their asset value rises. Producers of essential commodities also benefit during high inflation. Essential items are inelastic, and high prices mean high profit margins for the producers. Certain external factors, like geopolitical tensions, often lead to soaring crude oil prices. Oil companies, during such times, make heavy profits. To ensure fairness, the government imposes a type of tax on them, called the windfall tax.

If we take a bird's-eye view of this, we can conclude that it's the low-income households who are disproportionately affected by inflation, especially in the Indian context. For instance, food inflation is a major concern in India's economy. Around 46% of the household expenditure in rural areas and around 38% in urban areas is spent on food[4]. When such a large chunk of monthly expenses is going towards food alone, there's little share left for other expenses. Wealthier people tend to own diversified, inflation-protected assets that give greater returns during inflation, while, in contrast, the savings of the poorer sections, held mostly in cash, get eroded due to high inflation. This widens the already existing inequality in society. Have you ever wondered why the farmers don't benefit from the rising food inflation? This is because they are at the lower levels in the agricultural value chain, and have very limited bargaining power. It's the middlemen, traders, and large corporations who dominate and reap the most benefits.

## Policy Patterns: How To Deal With Inflation

There are two bodies responsible for handling inflation levels in the economy. One, the government, through what we call the Fiscal Policy. Second, the central bank of the country, through its Monetary Policy. To know exactly what measures they take, we will apply a reverse approach. We'll first understand what is the underlying aim of both policies to control inflation, and then move to the measures. We know that during inflation, demand is higher than supply. This means the target is to bring the aggregate demand close to the aggregate supply. For this, both the fiscal policy and monetary policy generally try to suck liquidity from the economy. Let's first see how the central banks do that.

Central banks deploy two types of tools, quantitative and qualitative, to reduce liquidity in the banking sector. One of the major ways through which people have money in their hands is through credit. Therefore, central banks target the credit supply in the economy. How do they do it? Just like we borrow from banks when we need money, banks borrow from the central bank when they need money. Central banks make such loans, given to banks, expensive. When banks borrow at higher interest rates, they, in turn, lend to their borrowers at higher rates. For businesses and retailers, loans become expensive. This discourages people from spending more money, thereby reducing the overall demand in the economy. If we take the case of India, the RBI increases the lending rates mainly through the Repo rate. This is the quantitative tool deployed by the central bank. Other quantitative tools include the Cash Reserve Ratio (CRR) and Statutory Liquidity Ratio (SLR) through which the RBI tweaks the liquidity available with the banks. This is discussed in greater depth in the 4th chapter, which is fully dedicated to the banking system. If we talk about the qualitative measures, the RBI uses methods of moral suasion, credit rationing, or direct action to influence sector-specific credit supply. These methods are instructive, suggestive, or directive in nature.

Now, let's come to the fiscal policy. To reduce liquidity levels in the economy, the government takes measures like increasing the taxes charged on businesses and people. Higher tax reduces the disposable income of the people. Disposable income is the money left in the hands of people after paying their taxes. Less money means less spending, thereby reducing the overall demand. The government might also reduce its own expenditure to reduce the level of money flowing into the economy. The role of government in liquidity injection is discussed in the 6th chapter. These measures are to adjust the demand levels in the economy. As we know that inflation can also happen due to supply-side constraints. Under such a situation, the government takes steps to enhance the production levels in the economy or any specific sector(s).

## Terms Ending with "Flation"

As we end our discussion on inflation, here's some bonus knowledge for you. If we break the term Inflation into two parts, we get "In" and "Flation". The latter is derived from the Latin word "Flatus," meaning blowing or inflating. In economic terms, it signifies the changes in price levels of goods and services. If you go through the economic sections of newspapers or read articles related to price levels in the economy, you will also encounter other terms that have "flation" in them. Some of these terms include deflation, disinflation, reflation, hyperinflation, skewflation, stagflation, and shrinkflation. Deflation is simply the opposite of inflation, i.e., a reduction in price levels. Disinflation is the reduction in the rate of inflation. In this, inflation is still happening, but at a rate lower than the previous rates. Reflation is the result of government policies to increase economic activity, often done to recover from an economic slowdown. Hyperinflation refers to an extremely high level of inflation, for example, inflation as high as 50% or even more. Under skewflation, prices of a certain set of goods increase while others may remain stable or witness deflation. It is also referred to as biflation. Shrinkflation is like a hidden inflation that helps companies not let their consumers feel the heat of inflation. This is a strategy where the price of the goods is kept the same even during inflation, but the quantity given is reduced. Have you observed that certain items you used to buy a few years back cost the same even today? How is it possible for companies to survive inflation without increasing their selling price? They can because they are reducing the size of their products. The quantity of noodles we got years back is not the same as what we get now. By now, you have a better understanding of the price changes. Let us now move to money and how it moves in the economy.


[1] Marginal Revolution University. (n.d.). *Zimbabwe's currency and hyperinflation*. Marginal Revolution University.

[2] Outlook Business. (2024, March 12). *10 Elon Musk tweets that created waves in crypto world*. Outlook Business.

[3] Contractor, F. (2022, February 18). *Inflation: Friend of the rich, enemy of the lower income earners*. The Times of India.

[4] Ministry of Statistics and Programme Implementation. (2024). *Household Consumption Expenditure Survey: July 2022 – August 2023 (Report No. 591)*. Government of India.

### CHAPTER FOUR

# SAVINGS, BANKING AND BEYOND

We started the last chapter with the piggy bank example. Let's talk more about this. As kids, we used to keep our pocket money in piggy banks. Have you ever wondered why those small enclosed boxes have the words 'piggy' and 'bank' in them? The original shape of piggy banks was actually that of a pig toy; however, over the years, the name has been associated with all such boxes, with different shapes and sizes, and is used to save money. The money boxes were mostly pig-shaped because, in ancient times, it was believed that pigs were a symbol of wealth and prosperity[1]. What about 'bank'? When we say "bank", we think of it as a body that keeps our money as deposits and lends it to us when needed. We know that the economy started with the barter system. In ancient days, wealth was associated with tangible goods - land, cattle, precious metals like gold, silver, etc. If we go back a little more, wealth meant the tools, food, and shelter for early man. Over the years, wealth has evolved from such tangible assets to more complex forms. With the transition from agriculture to industrialization, innovation and technological advancements have added more to our wealth basket. In today's time, apart from the physical assets, wealth also includes financial assets, like cash, bonds, stocks, etc. Don't worry! All these terms are not to scare you. The 5th chapter is dedicated to the different types of financial assets we can have. For now, we will stick to money and banking.

There's a famous dialogue in the movie *Deewar*, where the character of Amitabh Bachchan brags about his wealth, like buildings, property, and bank balance, to his brother. Here, our focus would revolve around the "bank balance". We started with piggy banks. But we are adults, so let's talk about the real banks. If your neighbour offers you his locker to keep your valuables, will you accept it? Most probably no! Why would you keep your valuables like money at your neighbour's house? You would go to a bank to keep them, just like everyone does. But do we question the bank? Why do we trust the banks with our money? Why does the bank give interest on keeping our money instead of charging rent? How does a bank earn money? If you know the answer to these questions, you can skip to the next section, but for beginners, here's a quick explanation: So what the bank does is that they take money from us in the form of various deposits. In banking terms, they can be classified as demand deposits (like savings and current accounts, from which money can be withdrawn at any time) and time deposits (like fixed deposits and recurring deposits - here, money can be withdrawn after a certain fixed time). This deposited money is then lent out to various borrowers who need some money. While lending out money, the banks charge a certain interest from the borrowers, say 8%. On the other hand, banks give interest to depositors for keeping their money with the bank. The interest on deposits is lower than the interest on credit. Here, in our example, let's say it's 5%. The difference in the interest rates, equaling 3% (8%-5%), is the profit or earnings of the bank. Woah! You just learned an important banking term - Net Interest Margin (NIM). This 3% is the NIM of the bank in our example.

In short, the more deposits with the bank, the more they can lend and thus, the more their profit. But here's an interesting question that might have struck your mind. If the banks are lending our money to someone else, isn't that risky? What if I, as a depositor, want to withdraw my money immediately? What will the bank do then? Will they ask the borrower to immediately pay back their loan so that they can give it to me? The answer is - No! This is because of something called Fractional Reserve Banking. We will come back to this in detail, but before we get to this complicated, or rather, not-so-complicated part, it would be interesting to first ponder how the banking system originated and eventually took the form that it is today.

## *Tracing Back: Evolution of Banks*

The banks that we see today and how they function were not the same in the past. The origin of banks can be understood from the word itself. "Bank" originates from the Italian word "Banco", which means "Table". There's another word, "Banque", which comes from France and has a similar meaning to "Bench". These words - table and bench were a reflection of the way the banking system worked during medieval times. Unlike modern banking institutions, there were moneylenders and traders who used to sit at money counters or tables from where they conducted their business of moneylending and financial transactions. This was probably the time of the Renaissance. However, the banking system in its crude form can be traced back even to ancient times. In those days, there was no concept of paper currency and regulations by any central banks like we have now. Temples in ancient civilizations of Mesopotamia, Egypt, and Greece acted as the earliest banks. Their main function was to safeguard people's valuables like grains, precious metals, etc. Examples of such temples include the Temple of Babylon and the Athenian Parthenon. As productivity and trade among regions increased, various individuals and small groups started emerging as moneylenders who would lend to traders and merchants. Medieval times witnessed further growth in the banking domain. Cities like Venice and Florence became hubs of trade that pushed for the emergence of merchant banking. There was a very famous bank called the Medici Bank of Florence, which was founded around the late 1300s. Innovative financial instruments were developed during those times, like the Letter of Credit and Bill of Exchange. These were provided to facilitate international trade[2].

Let's imagine there was a trader, John, residing in Venice. He had to buy pearls from a seller in another city, far away from Venice. To make payment for his trades, he had to carry a large number of coins in those days, which was very inconvenient. Therefore, he went to, say, Medici Bank in his city and paid them the required amount. In return, the banker gave him a bill of exchange, which is a promissory note. Now, instead of so many coins, John only has to provide the bill of exchange to the seller. The seller, upon receiving it, can redeem his payment from the local branch of Medici Bank - basically, the associates of Medici. Such instruments existed even in India, but with a different name. In India, it was called Hundi. Gradually, the banking system grew bigger and catered to diverse sections of people. From merchant banking to commercial banking and further to investment banking, the sector has expanded in its functioning.

If we talk specifically about India, traces of the banking system can be found in ancient texts like Arthashastra, where we can find mentions of words like "Rnapatra", which meant loan deeds, "Sreni", "Sarthavaha", "Karanas", "Adesha", "Hundi", etc[3]. Guilds acted as banks and trusts[4]. Shroffs were those who acted as financial intermediaries for managing deposits, providing loans, etc. With the coming of the Britishers in India, we saw the emergence of the earliest modern banks in India - the Bank of Hindustan. The Bank of Bengal, Bank of Bombay, and Bank of Madras - some of the earliest banks - were later merged into one bank - the Imperial Bank of India in 1921. This bank exists even today and is called the State Bank of India (renamed and nationalized in 1955).

## Fractional Reserve Banking: Behind the Scenes

Now that we have a brief idea of how the banking sector evolved over the years, it's time to explore the interesting part: the fractional reserve banking system. Let's understand this with the help of Mr. David and his two children. One day, Mr. David gave a ₹ 100 note to his elder child, Ria, as pocket money. Since Ria had no lined-up expenses, she kept them in the cupboard safely. The next day, her little brother, Rahul, came to her for money. He wanted to buy his favourite ice cream. Ria gave him ₹50 with a promise that he would return her money as soon as he got his pocket money. On his way to the ice cream shop, he found his friend Virat standing in front of a stationary shop. Virat's parents were out of town, and he was staying with his neighbours. Upon asking, Rahul came to know that Virat wanted to buy a pen, but he was hesitant to ask for money from his neighbours. Thus, Rahul gave him ₹25. Virat thanked Rahul and promised him to return those ₹25 when his parents would come back. At this point, assuming that both the kids, Rahul and Virat, would stick by their promise and return the money, we can consider this as their bank balances, which would be ₹100, ₹50, and ₹25 for Ria, Rahul, and Virat, respectively. On adding the three, the total bank balance of the three would equal ₹175. But hey! Actual cash was only ₹100, right, the one that Mr. David gave to Ria? Yes, and that ₹100 is called the base money in the banking world. Those ₹175 are the credit money. What led to the creation of money? What Ria and Rahul did is what the banks do. Banks lend out the money from the deposits they have to those who need it, with a promise of returning the money within a specified time. If you closely observe the amount lent by Ria and Rahul, you would see a similar pattern - the percentage of the money they lent is the same, 50%. They did not give the total amount to the other. This is because what if Ria wanted to buy something immediately, and asked for her money back from Rahul? Since Rahul has ₹25 with him, he can return at least that much for the time being. If you have understood this, you have cracked the basics of the modern banking system. Banks do not lend all of our deposits to others. They keep some reserve with them so that if any depositor wants their money back, they can give it. This is what we refer to as the fractional reserve system. It is because of this, the banks can create money out of thin air.

## *The Money Multiplier Effect: How It Works?*

The money multiplier effect helps us to calculate how much new money can be created from the base money in the economy. As of January 2025, the base money in India is approximately ₹46.5 lakh crores, whereas credit money is around ₹266 lakh crores. What does this mean? This means that the RBI has issued only ₹46 lakh crores of physical money, and this forms the base for the actual circulation of money in the economy, which amounts to ₹266 lakh crores. If we divide the credit money by the base money, we can conclude that every ₹1 is supporting ₹5.78 of the money supply in the economy. In technical terms, the base money is called M0, whereas the credit money is called M3. To calculate the money multiplier, we divide the M3 by M0. So far, so good.

Have you ever gone to a restaurant and eaten something so unique and delicious that you wondered how the chef would have prepared the dish? If you are among such people who think about the 'making of' everything, you are at the right place. Let's give a sneak peek into how this system works. Based on the economic activities, production level, and demand created, the RBI prints currency. This gets circulated in the economy through salaries, profits, rents, etc. When we get our salary, we deposit it in our bank. Whenever we want to buy anything online, we make a payment. This money goes to the seller's account. Do you think that the banks transfer the amount physically by carrying hard cash from one bank to another? The bank doesn't keep all this money idle. As discussed before, after keeping a certain amount as a reserve, they lent out the rest of the money. The loan money is deposited into the borrower's account. The borrower might have taken the loan to, say, buy a car. So the loan money is now transferred to the card dealer. Again, do the banks transfer physical currency from your account to the borrower to the car dealer's bank account? Doesn't this look like a postman carrying a letter from one person to another and then to another?

To simplify the lives of banks, transactions are not completely physical. Banks keep cash with them only to the extent required. Here's how the transactions are done - Banks are connected to all other banks through a common payment and settlement system controlled and regulated by the RBI. Banks are required to maintain a reserve account with the RBI. Payment and settlement happen through this reserve account. Just like we have our accounts opened with different banks, banks have their accounts with the RBI. The amount to be kept in such accounts is decided by the RBI. This is called the Cash Reserve Ratio (CRR). So if the CRR is, say, 4%, then a bank that has, say, a total deposit of ₹100 crores has to keep ₹4 crores in its reserve account. There's another kind of reserve that the banks need to maintain - Statutory Liquidity Ratio (SLR). This is to be kept by the banks with them. So whenever you go to a bank to take out money from your account in the form of hard currency (physical notes), you get it from the SLR. The sum of currency in circulation and reserves kept with the RBI forms the M0 or base money. Central banks of the economies tweak the reserve requirements (CRR and SLR) to influence the level of credit creation in the economy. For example, if too many people are depositing their money in bank accounts, the liquidity levels increase. Banks might start giving too much credit to people. Thus, the RBI can increase CRR. If deposits are low, banks would have less money to lend out. In this case, the RBI can lower the CRR to promote credit growth.

## *The Money Market: Saviour of the Banks*

The amount of deposits and credits keeps fluctuating. There are situations when banks run into a deficit, for instance, at the end of a financial year, employees and businesses have to clear tax settlements. Government expenditure, too, can influence liquidity conditions. Just like Rahul and Virat borrowed from their peer, banks also conduct interbank lending and borrowing for short-term liquidity requirements. Suppose ABC Bank has less money while XYZ Bank has surplus money. ABC Bank can borrow from XYZ Bank for durations ranging from 1 day to 1 year. Such short-term lending and borrowing among the banks and other investors come under what we call the Money Market. There are various instruments such as Call Money (for overnight borrowings), Notice Money (for 2-14 days), Repo agreements, etc. Here's a short nugget for you: If you ever feel curious about the liquidity conditions in the banking sector, just look for the short-term trends in the prevailing interest rates of these money market instruments. If interest rates are on the rise, overall liquidity conditions in the banking sector would be tight. Reason: basic demand and supply mismatch - more hands chasing fewer goods. Here, 'hands' refer to the banks that need money, and 'goods' are the surplus liquidity held by fewer banks. The opposite happens when there is surplus liquidity in the banking system - lower interest rates on money market instruments. Visualize this as a group of people with different levels of money. If a majority of the people in the group have excess money, they would agree to lend at lower interest rates because the borrower has too many options. However, if fewer people have excess money, they would charge higher interest rates because borrowers don't have many options.

## We Trust You: But Why?

We now know how the banks function better than before. But, don't you think there's a glitch in this system? What if everyone wants their money back, all at the same time? Will the banks be able to service their customers? Of course not. Such situations are called a Bank Run. Many bank runs have occurred in the past. Reason: Erosion of trust. The banking system stands tall due to the trust factor. People have faith in the bank to keep their hard-earned money with it. Neither the bank nor its customers, you and I, are doing any act of benevolence. As much as we need the banks, the bank needs us too. Banks earn profit as an intermediary between depositors and borrowers. How will the bank lend if they don't get the deposits? We need banks to protect our money from losing its value and earn interest on it. Also, it's difficult to keep physical money with us, especially if the amount is huge. Thus, even for safety purposes, banks are the primary option. So, if it is a give-and-take relationship, how does trust come into play? Have you ever taken a loan? Banks don't give loans to anyone and everyone. It does a lot of background checking. They check our past loan payment history through what is called a credit score. They see our earnings and salary slips to see if we are capable enough to pay them back or not. They keep collateral as security, so that, in case we fail to pay them back, they can seize it. What documents do we keep with us when we deposit our money with the banks? Do we ask for their credentials - show us your earnings, KYC-like documents (Know Your Customer), etc. No, right! Because we trust the banks. How does this trust develop?

Banks and all financial institutions are regulated and supervised by a dedicated institution - the central bank of the economy, the RBI in the case of India. The RBI is responsible for granting licenses to banks. Only those entities are given the banking license that fulfill certain minimum standards. The central bank ensures proper checks and balances to keep the banking sector stable and healthy. Due to regulatory obligations, all commercial banks are required to provide a deposit insurance cover of up to ₹5 lakh for a single bank (as of FY2024-25). The premium amounts for such deposit insurance are paid by the banks themselves. Deposit Insurance and Credit Guarantee Corporation (DICGC), a subsidiary of the RBI, is the dedicated body for such deposit insurance. So, in case a bank fails to fulfill its obligation and becomes bankrupt, our money will be recovered up to a maximum of ₹5 lakh. This is the worst possible situation that can arise. RBI makes sure that banks' financial health is maintained at all times. Some of the major standards set by the RBI are based on a set of international regulatory standards set by the Basel Committee on Banking Supervision (BCBS), called Basel Norms or Basel Accords. Basel, a city in Switzerland, is home to the Bank for International Settlements (BIS), which was established in 1930. The BIS serves as a bank for central banks, facilitating cooperation among them. Under the Basel norms, banks are required to maintain a minimum level of capital as a percentage of their assets (loans given out by banks are their assets). This is termed as Capital to Risk-weighted Asset Ratio (CRAR) or simply Capital Adequacy Ratio. The central bank also keeps a check on their Non-Performing Assets (NPA) levels to ensure that banks are getting back their money lent out as loans. NPAs refer to those loans that turn bad, meaning the borrowers are unable to pay them back. Banks are also required to keep a certain percentage of their capital aside as provisions to cover their losses due to NPAs - the amount required refers to the Provisioning Coverage Ratio (PCR). Do you know? In the Indian banking sector, if a borrower doesn't pay their principal or installments (Equated Monthly Installments or EMI) for 90 days, the loan is classified as NPA. There are three other classifications of loans: Special Mention Accounts-0 (SMA-0) for those loans whose payments are overdue for up to 30 days. SMA-1 if overdue for 31 to 60 days, and SMA-2 if overdue for more than 60 days but less than 90 days. Provisioning is required for SMAs as well.

Situations where Companies default on their loans, leading to higher NPAs for banks, are referred to as the Twin Balance Sheet problem. Balance sheet refers to the record of a company's assets, liabilities, and equity ownership. For Companies, the loan is a liability. Higher level of debt and the inability to pay them back affects their financial health. For banks, the loan is an asset. High NPA level means deterioration of banks' asset quality. Thus, the balance sheet of both companies and banks gets affected, calling it the twin balance sheet problem. For the recovery and settlement of loans, there also exist measures. Insolvency and Bankruptcy Law has been put in place to deal with issues of bad debts. Loans are restructured, for example, the duration for repayment of principal and interest is extended or reduced, and available assets of the borrowers are liquidated (sold through auction to recover the money). Remember the infamous Vijay Mallya case? To recover the loan amount, his villas, jets, cars, etc, were put up for auction. Bodies like the National Company Law Tribunal (NCLT), Debt Recovery Tribunals (DRTs), and Asset Reconstruction Companies (ARCs) are there that help manage the bad loans. ARCs are also called Bad Banks. This is because they are experts in managing the bad loans. Banks often sell their bad loans to ARCs, which then try to recover as much as possible, thereby shifting the burden from banks to the Bad banks.

## Banking System Beyond "Banks"

All this while, we have been talking about banks. But do only banks provide credit to the borrowers? Here, banks refer to the traditional types of banks that we generally see and that dominate the financial system. Apart from the traditional banks, which most of us know of, other categories of banks and financial institutions also exist in the market. Major categories of banks, specific to India, are: Cooperative Banks, Regional Rural Banks (RRBs), Local Area Banks (LABs), and the latest ones, called differentiated banks. Differentiated banks were introduced in India by the RBI in 2014. These are of two types, Small Finance Banks (SFBs) and Payment Banks. All these category of banks helps to expand the reach of banking services, especially to the underserved and remote areas of the economy, and cater to the specific needs of different segments of the economy. These complement the traditional banks to achieve the goal of financial inclusion in our country. They differ from each other in how they function and are regulated. For instance, cooperative banks are those that are owned, financed, and operated by their members, who are also the bank's customers. On the other hand, RRBs are established by the central government, the state government, and commercial banks, together, to cater to the rural areas, particularly the small, marginal farmers, rural labourers, artisans, etc.

Moving on from banks, there exist several Non-Banking Financial Companies (NBFCs). Within NBFCs, there are different categories, such as NBFC-CIC (Core Investment Companies), NBFC-MFI (Micro Financial Institutions), NBFC-HFCs (Housing Finance Companies), etc. NBFCs offer specialised services to specific sectors or individuals where the banks might not serve. These, too, are complementary to the banks in providing access to finance to people and businesses. They are often referred to as shadow banks because they perform bank-like functions but are not regulated like them. NBFCs are not subject to similar levels of strict regulations as banks.

There's one interesting concept that you wouldn't want to miss. Have you visited a local grocery store where few people buy things on credit? They keep buying from the shop with the promise to pay at the end of the month, all at once. Even businesses work like this - on credit. Think that you are a businessperson who sells cotton fabric to shirt manufacturing companies. One of your clients bought the fabric from you on credit, saying he will pay you after 3 months. So, you created an invoice (bill) stating the amount due, say ₹1 lakh, after 3 months. It so happened that you needed cash immediately to make further investments. What would you do in such a situation? Go to the bank for a loan, or ask your client to pay back immediately? Neither of the two options seems viable since taking a loan could be time-consuming, and your client wouldn't pay since the invoice has 3 months to be cleared. Well, there's a third alternative. What you do is convert that invoice into a legal document, in which you take a legal promise from your client to pay you back after 3 months. Now, this invoice has turned into a bill of exchange. You take this bill of exchange to a bank and ask for money. The bank gives you ₹9,95,000, discounting your bill at 5%. Now, after 3 months, your client will pay ₹1 lakh to the bank instead of you. Due to this system, you were able to get your money immediately at a cost of ₹5000 (5% of 1 lakh), while the bank made a profit of ₹5000, and your client got his due time to pay back the amount. It was a win-win situation for the three parties involved. This whole system is called Trade Discounting.

Now, let's say, you don't want to take the burden of converting your invoices into legal papers (bill of exchange). So, you straight away took your invoice and went to a non-banking financial company. The NBFC took your invoice and gave you ₹80,000 for now. After 3 months, when your client pays the NBFC ₹1 lakh, you would get ₹14,000 after a deduction of ₹6000 as a fee charged by the NBFC for its service. Such a service is called Factoring, and such NBCFs are called NBFC-Factors. The difference between trade discounting and factoring is that in the former, a bill of exchange is used to get immediate money, while in the latter case, invoices are used. Trade discounting is a type of loan. On the other hand, factoring involves selling of invoices to a third party, thereby shifting the burden of collecting the due amount to the third party - the Factor. Here, in our example, we used the banks for trade discounting and NBFC for factoring, only for our understanding. Both services can be provided by either of them. In India, we have a dedicated set of platforms for trade discounting for smaller enterprises that often run on low cash. Such platforms are called TReDS - Trade Receivables electronic Discounting System. (Invoices are also called Trade Receivables.)

So, you see, how vast is our banking system? In the broader financial system, the banking sector is just one part. There's another interesting part within the financial system: the financial market. Let us turn to this topic in our next chapter.

[1] The Financial Brand. (2010, September 6). *The history of piggy banks*. The Financial Brand.

[2] Britannica. (n.d.). *Bank: Historical development*. In *Britannica Money*.

[3] Bhargav, B. (n.d.). *Indigenous banking in ancient and medieval India*. D.B. Taraporevala Sons and Co.

[4] Kumar Thaplyal, K. (n.d.). *Guilds in ancient India (Antiquity and various stages in the development of guilds up to AD 300)*

### CHAPTER FIVE

# FINANCIAL MARKETS: INVESTMENT, RISK AND RETURN

In the last chapter, we discussed the banking system, which acts as an intermediary and allows us to protect ourselves from inflation by giving us a return on our deposits. Can we call such deposits with banks a form of investment? Well, we all thought keeping our money in banks was like saving money, right? So, why is investment written over here? Are savings and investment synonyms, or is there a difference? Have you ever thought about such a difference? Let's understand these basic aspects of economics and finance first before we proceed further. Saving and investment differ from each other in two aspects: first, the purpose/intent. Savings are done to store your money safely and ensure it's easily accessible (termed as liquidity in economics). Investment, on the other hand, is done to make your money grow over time and generate wealth for you. Second, stability and risk. Savings are stable with almost no to very low risk involved. You feel assured that your money is with you only, whereas investment involves risks. Since the return on investments is generally higher compared to the return on savings, the risks are also higher[1]. There's a general conception in finance where it's said that the higher the return you get, the higher the risk involved, and the lower the return, the lower the risk.

There's a famous dialogue said by the infamous Harshad Mehta's character (played by Pratik Gandhi) in the web series, *Scam 1992*, where he talked about the stock market as an investment option, recognizing the risks involved in such an investment. So, now you know that the returns you are getting on your bank deposits are to attract you to park your money with the banks, and also give you protection against inflation. Although there are savings options provided by banks that give us a decent return and many people go for such products as their investment choices. However, you must understand that we are not here to make you choose what you do with your money. We are here to understand such concepts so that you can view the economic and financial world in a better, rational, and more intelligent way. Neither am I a financial advisor, nor are you here for any financial advice. Now, back to our knowledge zone.

If I ask you to tell me the alternative option for investing money, what would be your answer? The majority of us would probably say the stock market. This is because the stock market is the most common market among us. When I say market, what image forms in your mind? Is it a marketplace where you go for grocery shopping? If yes, then you need to think broadly. In finance, markets are not any particular physical store but a concept used to refer to the trade, i.e., buying and selling of something. This "something" can vary depending on the type of financial market we are talking about. The stock market is one such type of financial market where buying and selling of stocks (also called shares, although there's a difference which will be discussed further) takes place. There are various other types of financial markets, and we will discuss them all, but before that, let's delve into this term, 'financial market', first.

## Banking and Financial Markets: The Two Pillars

We have already discussed banking in our previous chapter. They are important for credit creation in the economy. People like you and me save and take loans to fulfill our personal/professional goals. Enterprises and corporations take loans to invest in their businesses. The financial market, on the other hand, provides us with avenues to invest and raise money. Here's an interesting thing. Banks don't just rely on our deposits to lend; they raise funds from other sources as well, such as the money market, bond market, etc. It also happens that sometimes banks lend money to enterprises for long tenure (such as infrastructure companies, which take time to get their returns). In such cases, banks, instead of waiting for that many years to get back their money, raise capital through various financial markets. We will understand this in detail when we discuss the derivative market. Companies, too, instead of relying solely on loans for funding their expenses, raise funds from various financial markets like the share market, bond market, etc. For you and me (retail investors from here on), the financial market provides alternative options to mobilize our savings and generate wealth. To sum up, the financial market is an essential pillar for efficient capital allocation by helping connect those with excess capital to those who need capital.

There exist many types of financial markets: Money Market, Capital Market, Commodity Market, Bond Market, Forex Market, Derivative Market. Each of these markets has its own set of significance and relevance. However, the fundamental principle underlying each financial market is common: the Principle of supply and demand. Capital allocation within these markets happens through what we call financial instruments. These are like physical or virtual documents or contracts that act as a mutual agreement between two parties who trade them. These instruments are assets because they hold value. It acts as a claim on ownership of something or on future cash payment. A better term in the financial market is Security. Securities are a subset of the financial instruments that are primarily designed for trading. We will get more clarity on this as we proceed further. Let's start with the most well-known market, the share market.

## *Stock Plus Bond Equals Capital Market*

Remember, we discussed the money market in the last chapter. Unlike money markets, which provide short-term capital (short-term generally refers to one year), the capital market is for long-term capital allocation. Companies use this market to raise long-term funds. Within this market, there are two broad categories of the market: Stock/Share Market and the Bond/Debt Market. Let's understand these two markets with the help of a hypothetical company named XYZ Ltd, which is based in India. The company was started by two friends with a 50:50 partnership. The two friends invested ₹10 lakh each in the company. Within a year of sales, they wanted more capital to grow their business. They knocked on the doors of a bank to take a loan. Over a few years, they expanded their business to 20+ cities. Now, they were planning to go pan-India. For this, they wanted huge investments. So, instead of going for a loan, they decided to raise capital from various investors by diluting their ownership. Over many rounds of investment, they onboarded around 10 investors. Thus, the initial ownership of 50% with each of the two founders got diluted and distributed amongst the 12 members, each having ownership in proportion to their investment. Such investments fall under what we call venture capital. You must have seen television shows like Shark Tank, where such investments are raised in exchange for ownership.

After a few years of success, the company decided to expand its business even further, and this time, it decided to go public. This means they decided to raise money through a public offering. This route of capital raising is termed as an initial public offering, in short IPO. Through this, the ownership of a company goes to the public in general. The IPO is a part of the primary market. In the financial market, any new issuance of an instrument is part of the primary market, and its buying and selling (trading) happens in what we call the secondary market. Think of it as a farmer growing apples and selling them to you at ₹10/apple for the first time. When you bought an apple, it happened as part of the primary market. Now, you feel that the price of apples in the market is ₹15/apple, so you sell them to someone at that price and make a profit of ₹ 5/apple. The one who bought it at ₹15 can sell it to someone else, and so on. This trading, starting from your selling, comes under the secondary market.

So, the XYZ Ltd. company, which was once having only two-part ownership, now has multiple owners. Each unit of ownership of a company is termed a share. Let's say XYZ Ltd. now has 1 lakh shares. When the company came up with an IPO, you bought 2 shares of the company. So now, you have 0.002% ownership of the company. Now you know why the stock market is also called the share market. Trading of shares (unit of ownership of a company) is what happens in the stock market. In this example, you saw how a company doesn't just rely on its own capital but also resorts to various options available to it, from credit to venture capital to public listing. Once a company raises capital from the public through an IPO, it gets listed on a stock exchange. The stock exchange acts as an intermediary that connects buyers and sellers to trade various securities. It facilitates the trading in the secondary market after going public. Other stakeholders in the stock market include stock brokers, depositories, etc. Stock brokers are licensed agents who execute the trades on our behalf, while depositories are institutions where our securities are held in electronic form, which is referred to as dematerialized form, in short, demat. That is why you would be asked to open a demat account in case you wish to start investing in the stock market.

Stock markets are also called equity markets because shares of a company are nothing but equity or ownership part of the company. Here's another aspect of the share market: If you take the case of banks lending capital to borrowers, there is an obligation to pay it back; however, in equity, there is no such obligation for the companies to pay back the capital they raised from the share market. Although they do have a choice in the form of what is termed as 'buybacks'. This means that companies can buy back their shares from their current owners. You might think, then, how will the investors profit if they don't get their money back along with any interest? Well, in the share market, the return is in the form of a change in the value of each unit of share. So if you bought 2 shares of XYZ Ltd. at ₹50, over a period of time, the value may appreciate to, say, ₹55, and thus, you made a profit of ₹10 (5*2). But for this, you have to sell your shares in the secondary market. Some other buyers, instead of the company, will buy from you.

You must also know that in the share market, there are times when we might not be able to sell (or even buy) the shares of certain companies. This happens when there are upper/lower circuits on such stocks. Too much volatility or poor performance of certain stocks creates illiquid conditions in their trades, leading to the unavailability of buyers/sellers. Therefore, we must know about the companies, their performance, financial health, and governance quality, before investing in their stocks.

Now, let's move to the second category of the capital market, the bond market. What if I tell you that just like banks and other lending institutions give credit to companies and consumers, we, too, give loans, in the form of an investment, to companies and even the government. Wait, what? We, giving loans to big companies and the government! When did that happen? Well, this happens through the bond market. Let's draw some parallels with the bank loans to understand this. When a bank gives us loans, it's a sort of investment for them. This is because they charge interest on loans, which we have to pay back after a certain duration. Similarly, various entities like companies and the government issue bonds. It's like a paper where the amount of money they want is written, and the interest they are willing to pay on that money is also written, along with the time duration for which they want the money before they return it. This is why bonds are also called debt securities. Companies, financial institutions, or the government issuing bonds are, in a way, raising money through borrowing. Unlike the stock market, where there is no fixed return date, bonds have a fixed date called the maturity date. The interest given is called the coupon rate. Coupon rates can be fixed or keep changing. The latter ones are called floating coupon rates.

Let's take the case of XYZ Ltd only. Suppose the company doesn't want to go through the long and stringent procedure of banks to borrow funds for their expansion, so they can go to the bond market to borrow. Bonds issued by companies are called corporate bonds. The government mostly borrows through this route. Bonds issued by the government are called Government Securities or G-sec in short. There are various categories of G-secs issued by the government - two broad categories are: one, T-bills or Treasury bills, which are short-term securities with a maturity period of less than one year. In India, there are 3 types of T-Bills issued by the Union government: 91-day T-bills, 182-day T-bills, and 364-day T-bills. These numbers are nothing but the maturity period. Second, Dated Securities, which are longer tenure bonds, have a maturity above one year. Did you know that till recently, retail investors were not allowed to invest directly in G-secs in India. Now, even retail investors can directly trade G-secs through the RBI.

The bond market in India is dominated by G-secs. The corporate bond market is not yet as developed as in developed economies. Corporations also issue bonds to borrow from foreign investors. One such bond is called the Masala bond. These bonds are denominated in Rupees (Indian currency), meaning the capital is raised in ₹ and not any foreign currency. This helps the issuers to protect themselves from exchange rate fluctuations. Even urban local government, the Municipalities in India, have started resorting to bonds to raise funds for their governance and developmental works. Such bonds are called Municipal Bonds. To provide liquidity for bond investors, i.e., to enable them to buy and sell bonds easily, many bonds also trade in the secondary market. When talking about the bond market, you would hear many addressing it as the fixed-income market. This is because, unlike the stock market, where you don't know the exact return, bonds or debt securities are pre-determined instruments in terms of their returns. So, a bond with a face value of say, ₹100 with a coupon rate of 5% and maturity of 1 year would give us ₹105 (₹100+ ₹5 interest) at the end of one year. However, there's a small twist to this return. Just now, we discussed that most bonds are traded in the secondary market as well. This means that the price of a bond would keep changing depending on its demand in the market. Let's say the ₹100 bond is trading at ₹90 in the secondary market due to low demand. Now, for someone who buy this bond from secondary market, instead of primary, would incur a cost of ₹90 but would get ₹5 as interest since interest is always calculated on the face value (face value is the price of the bond its issuer promise to give you at the time of its maturity). In terms of percentage, the gain would be around 5.5.% instead of 5%(5/90*100). This overall return on your investment is termed as bond yield. In other words, while coupon rates remain the same, bond yield keeps changing due to changing prices. The fixed income we are talking about is the fixed return calculated on coupon rates and not the actual earnings. Here, in our example, ₹5 would be the fixed return, no matter what price the bond is being traded at, in the secondary market.

## Tell Me More: Capital Market Bonus

Sometimes companies offer bonus shares to their shareholders when they earn some extra profit. This section is just like those bonus shares. Let's get started. Whenever a listed company makes a profit, they have two options: either reinvest those profits back into the company or give a share of the pie to its shareholders as well. After all, the shareholders are also part-owners of the company. This sharing of profit with shareholders is called dividends. Let's say XYZ Ltd. made a profit of ₹10 lakh in a financial quarter (A financial year has 4 quarters). This ₹10 lakh would be distributed to 1 lakh shareholders (same as mentioned before). Therefore, you having 2 shares of the company would have gotten ₹20 as a dividend (10 lakh/1 lakh*2). Such dividend distributions are not mandatory for companies. If you see or read stock market news, you would often come across terms like Nifty, Sensex. What are these? These are nothing but a performance metric measuring a bunch of shares together. The term for this is Index (Plural - Indices). Think of Index as a basket containing a bunch of a particular type of asset. While Nifty Index tracks the top 50 companies listed on the stock exchange of NSE (National Stock Exchange), Sensex tracks the top 30 companies listed on BSE (Bombay Stock Exchange). How do we rank the companies, then? Companies are ranked based on their market capitalisation. It's calculated by multiplying the current price of one unit of share trading on the stock exchange by the total number of shares. So, the hypothetical market capitalisation of XYZ Ltd. would be 1,00,000 multiplied by 250 (considering its current share price is ₹250), which is equal to ₹ 2.5 crores. (These numbers are taken for ease of understanding and calculation. There are various rules regarding conditions for a company to be listed, like minimum capital requirement, profitability, minimum market capitalisation, etc.)

Equity and debt markets have various channels through which we can put our money. Mutual funds are one such channel where many people's investments are pooled together and then invested in different equity and debt securities, depending on the return expectations and risk appetite of the investors. Each investor in a mutual fund invests some money that could be one time or at regular intervals. The latter ones are called a Systematic Investment Plan (SIP). Another fund similar to a mutual fund is, Alternative Investment Fund (AIF). The difference here is that the minimum investment required to be invested in AIFs is ₹1 crore (in India), and thus, such funds are generally for people considered as High Net-worth Individuals (HNIs). For mutual funds in India, as of FY2024-25, the minimum investment can be as low as ₹100 in lump sum (i.e., one-time). Such pooling of funds is done for other types of investments as well, for instance, Real Estate Investment Trusts (REITs) and Infrastructure Investment Trusts (InvITs). Here, instead of investing in shares and bonds, investments are made in properties and infrastructure projects like roads, rail, and ports, without direct ownership. Exchange Traded Funds, or ETFs, are similar to mutual funds, but here, the funds passively track a specific index or asset, unlike in mutual funds, where there are fund managers who actively decide where to put the pooled money to gain maximum returns. ETFs are always traded on stock exchanges, so you can buy and sell them anytime you want. Coming to one last interesting thing: There are certain bonds that can turn into shares of a company. Yes, you heard that right! Such bonds are called convertible bonds. So you may lend money to a company, and over time, you would get ownership in the company through the shares equivalent to the value of your investment in such bonds.

## *Money Market: The Opposite of Capital Market*

While the capital market is for long-term investment and fundraising, the money market is the place you go for a short-term duration, which is generally one year or less. Companies and financial institutions need capital not just for expansion and scaling. They require money for day-to-day operations as well. Such requirements are termed as working capital. We already discussed a few of the money market instruments used by banks for financing their day-to-day liquidity deficits in the 4th chapter. Companies, too, can raise short-term capital using instruments like commercial papers (CPs). In India, CPs are unsecured, meaning it is not backed by any collateral. When we take loans from the banks, we generally have to give collateral as security so that in case of any default (inability to pay back the loan due), banks take the collateral to recover their money. Such loans are called secured loans. The minimum value of a CP in India is ₹5 lakh, and it can be issued in multiples of 5 lakh, e.g., ₹10 lakh, ₹15 lakh, ₹20 lakh, and so on.

## The Complex Derivative Market

Remember when we were toddlers, we used to play doctor-doctor or with our kitchen-set toys. We derived pleasure from such activity without actually learning anything about medicine or cooking. Then we grew up and realised that such games are not real. We have to study hard and learn to acquire such a degree or skills. We knew we were grown-ups when we were introduced to the world of variables in maths. The "Let x=y+4" kind of questions took us to a different world. What's interesting in these maths questions is that the value of one variable is derived from some other variable or an equation. Here, every time you change the value of y, you will get a new value of x. In simple words, the value of x is derived from the value of y. Similar to the above two instances where we were deriving some value from the other, derivatives as financial instruments also derive their values from what we refer to as the underlying asset, or simply an 'underlying'. In technical terms, derivatives are contracts whose value is derived from any asset, be it equity/shares, bonds, indices, commodities, currency, or even interest rates. Just like x is deriving its value from 'y+4', derivatives also derive their value from something that has a return value. You might question why we need such securities or financial instruments which doesn't have a value of their own but depend on some assets, and why we need such instruments when we can directly trade the underlying asset instead of its derivative. To answer this question, we need to understand the various types of risks involved in the financial market. But before that, we must know that there are mainly four types of derivative instruments: Forwards, Futures, Options, and Swaps. We will understand each of them one by one.

Have you ever organised an event or witnessed someone in your family organise functions like a marriage or a birthday party? You would observe that they would book venues, catering services, etc, in advance. Such advance bookings are done for two main reasons. One, to avoid last-minute unavailability of such services, especially in case of marriages which happen during peak wedding seasons. Second, to avoid price escalations due to high demand. Pre-booking involves giving an advance or token money to reserve your place. This way, people protect themselves from price volatility. If you come to know today that the prices of onions are going to escalate in the coming days, you would buy and store onions today itself. Such fluctuations in price are called market risk in the financial world. Derivatives emerged to avoid such market risks. To your wonder, the derivative market is not a new thing. It emerged thousands of years ago when farmers and traders traded in such instruments. Imagine a farmer cultivating cotton feels that the demand for cotton after its harvest season would drop, leading to a fall in the market price. This means he would get a lower price for his produce. Let's specify some numbers for better clarity. At the time of sowing, the market price is ₹100 per kg of cotton. There are talks in the town that the price could drop to ₹80 per kg. There's a trader who is ready to pay him ₹110 per kg at the time of harvest, irrespective of the prevailing market price. Thus, the farmer and trader enter into a contract fixing the selling price of cotton at ₹110. After the harvesting, they execute the deal. There could have been two scenarios in this situation. First, the price dropped to say ₹80. In this case, the farmer protected himself from the loss of ₹30 while the trader bore the loss. The second scenario could have been the opposite. Instead of a drop, the price soared to ₹120. In this case, the farmer earned ₹10 less for every kg while the trader made a profit of ₹10 per kg. However, the farmer still made sure he sold his produce at a reasonable rate. Such contracts are termed as forwards. What the farmer was doing in the name of protecting his earnings is called hedging in finance. So if the farmer was hedging, what was the trader doing? Why did he enter into the forward contract? The trader was speculating. This means he was trying to make a profit out of the price fluctuations in the market. He made a bet on a price rise by agreeing to buy at ₹110. Maybe, he would have thought the cotton price would rise to ₹120, thereby allowing him to make a profit of ₹10 per kg (His cost price being ₹110 and selling price ₹ 120).

In one line, forwards are derivative contracts for buying and selling an asset at a future date at a pre-determined price. Many companies, big and small, enter into forward contracts to hedge their earnings. Many airline companies hedge through forward contracts. This is because the aviation sector is highly dependent on crude oil prices, or simply fuel, for flying. High fuel price volatility can cost airlines huge losses. Thus, they pre-determine the fuel prices in advance to reduce their losses. Forwards have a sister derivative, called Futures. Future derivatives are almost the same as forwards, with a few differences. Futures are standardised contracts traded on a regulated exchange like the NSE or BSE, while forwards are privately placed, referred to as Over-the-counter (OTC). Since forwards are traded outside of exchanges, they are riskier than futures. What if the other party backs off from executing the contract? This, technically, is called counterparty risk. In futures, we need to pay a margin money as a guarantee deposit. We will come back to futures again when we discuss the forex market.

Moving on to Options. I remember when I read about options for the first time, it took me so much time to comprehend them. But then, I happened to experience something that replicated the options. So, before we discuss the actual options, hear me out with a personal incident. Recently, I was booking a flight ticket online. As you may know, the flight ticket price keeps fluctuating (demand and supply game), so many ticket booking platforms provide a feature of locking the price of the tickets. The booking was for an international trip for my brother. Since he was busy with his work, he had asked me to book for him. However, his travel plans weren't yet confirmed, and so there was a 50-50 chance of him travelling. You may know that international flights are expensive, but they keep fluctuating depending on the timings and days on which you are booking. On some days, prices are shown damn expensive while on some lucky days, you could get it cheap. When I checked the ticket fare, it wasn't too expensive, so I thought of booking it then and there. But there was a problem. Such cheaper tickets come with a clause: They are non-refundable. Since my brother wasn't 100% sure of his travel plans, I couldn't book the ticket immediately. However, I knew that I wouldn't get the flight tickets at that price after a few days. So I used the feature of Price-lock. This required me to pay a nominal non-refundable fee. I did this so that in a few days, even if the price rose, I would still be paying the locked price. In case his plans got cancelled or if the price went down even further, I would let go of the booking. My only loss would be the nominal fees I paid. Within a few days, I found out that his plans were postponed. So I didn't complete the booking transaction. But, the interesting thing was that while canceling my transaction, I checked the fare for that day, and it had soared very high. Had his plans not been cancelled, I would have flaunted my smartness to him for saving so many bucks.

Now that you know how to be a smart risk-taker, let's dive into options. Options are similar to the price-lock feature we just talked about. Just like the price-lock feature, where we have to pay a nominal fee, options provide us with a feature where we can hold the right to buy or sell an asset without actually owning it. They just give you the right to trade the assets by paying some nominal fee, which, in options, is referred to as the premium. These derivative instruments give the buyer the right, without an obligation, to buy or sell an underlying asset at a specific price, called the strike price. Let's break it down further. We know that when there is a buyer, there has to be a seller. While the buyer has the right without an obligation to execute the trade, the sellers have an obligation if the buyer executes. In my anecdote, the booking platform was obligated to confirm my ticket at the locked price had I completed the transaction. While I had the freedom to book or cancel, the platform wasn't allowed to refuse. There are two types of options:

Call and Put. In both types, there are buyers as well as sellers. The difference between the two arises due to the difference in the expectations of the buyers and sellers. Let's suppose a hypothetical company XYZ Ltd. is listed on a stock exchange, and we are going to take this company's shares as the underlying asset for the options derivative. Let the current share price of the company be ₹2500. I made some analysis of this company's performance and feel that its share price would go up in the near future, so I see an opportunity to earn profits. Now, I have two choices. First, I can buy its shares at ₹2500 and wait for it to spike. But the problem is that I only have ₹50,000 with me. With this much money, I would get 20 shares. If the price rises to ₹2700, I will make a profit of ₹4000 (200*20).

Now, let's come to the second choice, which is buying options. Instead of buying the shares (the actual asset), I only buy the right to buy the asset at a pre-determined price, here, say, ₹2500, by paying ₹50 per share as a premium. Options are traded in lots, meaning you can buy the rights of a bunch of shares (called lot size) and not individual shares. So, if the XYZ Ltd. Call Options have a lot size of 100, then I have to pay ₹5000 for 1 lot (50*100). Since my budget is ₹50,000, I can buy 10 lots (50,000/5000), meaning I will get the rights over 1000 shares. My strike price, as mentioned before, was ₹2500. So, now, if the share price goes up to ₹2700, my profit margin would be ₹2 lakh (200*1000) and when I sell them at ₹2700, my final (net) earnings would be ₹2 lakh minus the premium paid (₹50,000), which is ₹1.5 lakh. In the first choice, I was making a profit of ₹4000, while in the second choice, it was ₹1.5 lakh with the same amount of investment. This sounds so revolutionary, right? Did we discover the path to richness? Well, we need to calm down a bit because this is just an over-simplified explanation of the basics of options. Things are much more complicated in actual trade, which you wouldn't want to know at this point to keep your sanity intact. Coming back to this, the above case was when we were bullish (expecting a price rise) about XYZ Ltd. During bullish expectations, the buyers buy call options. What if you think the company's share price may go down (bearish view)? In this case, you can buy Put Options. In put options, the buyers buy the right to sell the shares at a pre-determined price (strike price), and when the price actually goes down, they buy those shares. Wait, what! Sell first and then buy? How can we sell something before buying it? Remember, we are just talking about the "right" to buy or sell and not the actual buying or selling. So, in a put option, the buyer gets the right to sell at, say, ₹2500, and if the price goes down to ₹ 2400, they buy it. What went out of their pocket is the premium for buying the right to sell, and what came into the pocket is the difference in the prices, ₹100 per share (2500-2400).

In both the scenarios (bullish and bearish), we discussed them from the buyer's side. There's also the seller side, where traders make money if the market goes opposite to what the buyers were expecting. They would then earn from the premium that the buyers had to forgo. However, if the market goes as per the expectations of the buyers, the sellers would make huge losses. Thus, it is said that the losses of the buyer side are limited (only up to the premium paid) while there can be no limits to the losses for the seller side. (In our example, the price could have risen even above ₹2700). These are some of the basic understandings of options. There's an interesting dialogue from the classic movie *Trishul* where legendary actor Amitabh Bachchan had come to make a deal with the character (played by Sanjeev Kumar), worth lakhs of rupees, despite him not having enough capital at that point, in the scene.

That dialogue fits so well in our understanding of derivatives, particularly options. With little or no money of his own, he is entering into a contract of such a big amount, just like in options, where we buy the rights to buy or sell an asset with little money. There's a term for such a concept in finance - Leverage. Leveraged instruments are those that allow investors to hold large positions (access to high levels of assets as underlying) with relatively smaller investments. This has the potential to aggravate investors' profits or losses. The leverage we just talked about is particular to the derivative market. There's another general meaning of leverage in finance. Sometimes, you might come across investors or financial institutions making investments from borrowed money. For instance, a company wants to invest in XYZ Ltd., whose current share price is ₹2500. To buy 400 shares of XYZ, it would need ₹10 lakh (2500*400). However, the company has only ₹5 lakh in hand. So, it borrows the rest ₹5 lakh and adds to its own capital. When the price reached ₹2600, the company sold those 400 shares and got ₹10,40,000, thus making a profit of Rs 40,000 (100*400). Out of this, ₹5 lakh needs to be returned back along with some interest. Let's assume that the interest charged was 2%, meaning the company had to return ₹5 lakh plus ₹10,000. After clearing the debt, the company is still left with a profit of ₹ 30,000 (40,000-10,000). Now, if we calculate the return percentage, it would be the net profit of ₹30,000 as a percentage of ₹ 5 lakh, which is 6%. Had the company invested 100% of its own capital (= ₹10 lakh), the profit would have only been 4% (40,000/10,00,000*100). Now, reversing this scenario. Let's say instead of a rise, the share price of XYZ Ltd. fell to ₹2400. This means a loss of ₹40,000, meaning after selling those 400 shares, the company would get only ₹9,60,000. After paying off the debt of ₹5 lakh plus the interest of ₹10,000, the company is finally left with Rs 4,50,000. The net loss of ₹50,000 (5 lakh minus 4.5 lakh), as a percentage, will be calculated on its own capital, and will be equal to 10% (50,000/5,00,000*100). Had the company invested 100% of its own capital, the loss percentage would have been only 4% (40,000/10,00,000*100). So, you saw how leveraging changes one's profit and loss margin. Here, leveraging enhanced the profit from 4% to 6%. On the other side, it brought down the loss from 4% to a whopping 10%.

After the scary options, let's discuss the last category of derivatives: Swaps. Swaps are as sweet as they sound. Its understanding also goes with the literal meaning of the word. In swaps, there is an exchange of some underlying assets or cash flow. Think of yourself and your colleague. Both of you took a loan from different banks. Your bank charges you a fixed interest rate of 7% while your colleague's bank charges her a floating interest rate. Floating rates are those that keep changing due to a variable rate attached to them, generally called the benchmark rate. As and when the benchmark rate changes, so do the floating interest rates. Currently, your friend's floating rate is 8%. Now, you are of the belief that in the coming days, this floating rate will drop to 6.5%. This is making you grow anxious, for you will still have to pay 7% interest, but your colleague will pay just 6.5%. However, your colleague is always scared of her interest rates. Since it keeps changing, she is fearful that if the rates go up to, say, 9%, it will cost her more in the future. In fact, she is actually envious of you for having a fixed interest rate of 7%, since you don't have to worry about the rise and fall. Upon seeing the two of you worried, a common friend suggested to exchange your interest rates with each other. So, now, you will pay as per the floating rate while your colleague will pay the fixed 7%. This is the whole story of swaps. Any of the two parties would be at a loss depending on the change in floating interest rates. If the floating rates fall to 6.5%, you will be the winner while your colleague would be at a loss, although it would only be 0.5%. On the flip side, if the floating rates go up to 9%, you would be at a loss of 2% while your colleague would gain a 1% benefit.

Swaps can be of various types. The above example was the case of interest rate swaps. There are currency swaps where the two parties exchange two different currencies to hedge against the fluctuating exchange rates. Then, there can be commodity swaps, where only the price difference of the commodities is exchanged (fixed price with floating price of a commodity). There's another type of swaps which got us crying during the 2008 global financial crisis, and that is: Credit Default Swaps, in short, CDS. However, unlike the other swaps, CDSs are not exactly an exchange of cash flow or assets. Here, there are three parties. A lender, a borrower, and a third party. Let's say there's a bank called ABC Bank. This bank has invested in the bonds issued by the company XYZ Ltd. The ABC Bank is fearful of a default by XYZ Ltd. What if the company goes bankrupt at the time of its bond maturity? This fear of the bank takes it to a third party, who's a risk taker. This third party could be anyone who has capital. The third party assures the ABC Bank to cover the risk in case of a default. In other words, if XYZ Ltd. fails to pay back the bank's investment at the time of maturity, this third party would pay the due amount to the bank. In return, the bank would be required to pay an annual premium amount as a fee for such guarantee. This premium would be decided by the third party depending on the probability (chances) of default. Higher default chances would mean higher premiums, while less risky bonds would require less premium. Here, the swap is of the credit risk and premium. The bank is buying the protection while the third party is selling the protection.

CDS, thus, acts like an insurance cover to protect against credit defaults. During the 2008 financial crisis, banks had bundled subprime credits into a derivative contract and converted them into CDS. Investors who bought these CDS, thinking they were safe, ended up paying for the defaults of the underlying subprime credits. Subprime credits are those whose chances of defaulting are very high. If a bank gives a loan to those with poor capacity to repay the loan, such loans are called subprime. Creditworthiness is measured through credit scores. But why would banks lend to people with low credit scores in the first place?

Now that we have touched upon the 2008 crisis because of CDS, let's go back to the days uncovering how we ended up with one of the biggest financial crises the world witnessed[2]. In the 3$^{rd}$ chapter on Inflation, we looked at how the policy rates set by central banks on behalf of the government influence the market interest rates. Pre-2008 crisis, the US central bank, the Federal Reserve, had lowered interest rates, thereby making borrowing cheaper. Banks during those days were lending housing loans at very low interest rates. This affordability led many people to buy houses on loans. We know the concept of demand-pull inflation - higher demand leads to a higher price. Real estate prices shot up too much. However, people were overoptimistic about the sector. The larger perception was that housing prices could never fall. This created a bubble. A bubble in the financial market refers to the overpricing of any asset to such a level that it could crash at any moment. Banks kept on lending home loans even to subprime borrowers. But wait, how did the banks get so much money to lend? This is where the derivatives come into the picture. Banks created derivative contracts whose underlying assets were these home loans. Yes, for the banks, loans are their assets since they earn interest on them. For the sake of simplification, let's say a bank had lent ₹20 lakh to 100 people. Thus, they have an asset of ₹20 crores on which they would get a return in the form of interest. However, the issue is that it would take some time for the banks to get back their money (Loans have a time period over which they are repaid). In other words, these ₹20 crores are locked in for a few years. So, to get their money back immediately so that they can lend to further people, they clubbed these loans together and created a derivative called MBS - Mortgage-Based Security (Mortgage is another word for a loan). Such MBS had values equivalent to the home loan assets that the banks had lent. Here, we take its value to be ₹20 crores. Banks traded such MBS to investors who thought them to be safe investment options since people would repay their home loans. However, since the MBS were backed by subprime loans, there were chances of default. This led the MBS investors to insure their investments through CDS. Those who bought these CDS to provide risk cover didn't have enough to cover the risk in case of defaults.

A bubble is a bubble. If you visit a fair and see a long line in front of a shop selling pencils for     ₹1, you may want to buy them even if you didn't want to. But, as the crowd increases, the shopkeeper would start raising their price. Demand-supply mismatch. After a point, the price could go up to, say,     ₹50, and people would start realising that the true value of this small pencil isn't that much. This would stop people from buying them and soon, its price would crash to what its true worth is. That's exactly what happened to the real estate sector pricing in 2006-2007. As the bubble of inflated prices started to fall back, people started defaulting on their home loans. This started a chain reaction. Home loan defaults meant the value of MBS crashed. Defaults in MBS meant huge claims on CDS buyers who provided a risk cover for the MBS. Since the CDS buyers didn't have enough money to pay the MBS holders, they started defaulting, too. Lehman Brothers, one of the biggest investment banking firms, had invested huge money in MBS and CDS. They had to file for bankruptcy (a legal process where a company declares its inability to pay back its debt, thus demanding debt relief from its creditors). All this created panic across the whole financial market. The stock market crashed as investors started selling their shares. The interconnectedness of the financial market across the globe extended the impact across many countries.

What aggravated this crisis were the speculations/bets on rising housing prices. Instead of using derivatives like MBS and CDS for hedging their risk, they started using them for high-risk gambling. People started buying multiple properties with borrowed money, with expectations of higher returns from high property prices. Financial institutions like hedge funds, pension funds, and foreign funds bought risky subprime loan-backed MBS. Some speculators sensed the bubble and started short selling (short selling refers to the trading where people borrow shares to sell at a specific price, hoping for a fall in the price, thereby buying at lower prices to make profits). So, does this mean speculating is bad for the economy? Not really. Speculation has an important role in the financial market. In the absence of speculators, there would be little liquidity in the market for the hedgers to reduce the chances of their loss. It also helps in finding fraud in financial sectors, since speculators keep an eye on the financial assets to see if they are overvalued or not. To summarise everything, we discussed the four types of derivatives: forwards, futures, options, and swaps. Then we also discussed the need for derivatives: hedging and speculating. There's one more benefit that derivatives offer us: Arbitrage, although this benefit is not limited to just the derivative market and can be observed in other financial markets as well.

In simple words, arbitrage refers to the practice of profiting from simultaneously buying and selling of same asset or asset class due to some temporary discrepancies in its prevailing prices in two different markets. Let's say that gold in New York is trading at $100 per gram while its price in India, at the same time, is ₹ 8400. How do we know if there's an arbitrage opportunity here? If you equate the price to one currency, you will know. Let's say that the current $/ ₹ exchange rate is 83, meaning 1$= ₹83. ₹8400 would then be equal to $101.20 (8400/83). Here, the arbitrage opportunity equals $1.2 (101.20 minus 100). This means, if we buy 1000 grams of gold from New York and simultaneously sell 1000 grams of gold in India, we will earn a profit of $1200 (1.2*1000). In rupees, it would amount to ₹99,600 (1200*83). So you see how a small window of opportunity was created due to the price difference at two different locations. That's arbitrage for you. Such price differences can happen due to various reasons across multiple markets. Traders keep looking for such arbitrage opportunities to make money. With this, we come to the end of the non-exhaustive derivatives market. If you have reached this far, give yourself 10 points, for you have reached the first level in understanding derivatives. But this is just the beginning. There are tens and hundreds of levels more to this. For now, we will move to the largest financial market in the world (in terms of trading volume). Any guesses?

## The Currency Market: Foreign Exchange

Foreign Exchange refers to the rate at which we exchange two currencies. Every country has its own currency, which is the legal tender, meaning, backed by their country's central bank. For instance, India has the Rupee (INR), the USA has the Dollar (USD), the United Kingdom has the Pound sterling, Japan has the Yen, and so on. When we buy things within our country, we exchange our domestic currency for the goods or services we buy. However, why would a lady from Japan accept money in rupees if she buys something from India? This takes us to the need to hold currencies of different countries to enable trade with them. The world has so many countries, and every country trades with so many different countries. Is it possible to keep every country's currency with us? No, foreign trade happens using just a few currencies - those that are easily acceptable and have high credibility in the market. Currently, it's the US dollar that holds the dominance in the currency market. Since the US is the most dominant economy, its financial market, especially its government bond market, is considered the safest. Almost every country compares the value of its currency to that of the US dollar. When we discussed arbitrage, I took the hypothetical exchange rate of USD/INR as 83. This tells the value of dollars in terms of rupees. How much do we need to pay in terms of rupees to buy 1 dollar? This exchange rate keeps changing depending on the demand for dollars and rupees in the global market. If the demand for dollars increases, the rupee will depreciate, meaning the exchange rate would go up above 83, to, say, 85. So, now to buy $1, we would need to pay ₹85. When the rupee depreciated, the dollar appreciated, because changes in the exchange rate happen in relative terms. The forex market deals with such exchange rate fluctuations. It provides a marketplace for buying and selling different currencies. Anyone needing to buy or sell one currency for the other has the forex market as their go-to place. Banks, financial institutions involved in lending and borrowing in different currencies, exporters, and importers involved in trading across borders, are all major participants in the forex market.

Within the forex market, we have three categories of markets: spot market, forward market, and futures market. Spot market involves the immediate trade of currencies at the current prevailing exchange rate, called the spot price. Forward and future markets are the derivatives within the forex market where parties to the contract trade currencies at a future date at a specific price. Exporters/Importers are highly vulnerable to exchange rate fluctuations. Imagine yourself as an importer based in India who buys raw cotton from the overseas market. You place an order from a US-based manufacturer for 1000 kg of raw cotton, at a time when the prevailing exchange rate of USD/INR is 81. If one shirt has an MRP of $3, it would cost you ₹243 per shirt (81*3). However, the order will be ready in 2 months. What if the rupee depreciates to 83/$ in 2 months? Instead of you paying ₹2,43,000 for the whole consignment, you would now have to pay ₹2,49,000, costing you ₹6000 extra. This is called currency risk, and to reduce such potential losses, traders often enter into forward or futures contracts to hedge their currency risks. For instance, oil refineries enter into forward contracts with crude oil producers to buy them at a pre-determined price at a future date to avoid the risk of exchange rate volatility, since cross-border trades take place in currencies different from their domestic ones. Even banks, financial institutions, and companies, having exposure in foreign investments or debt, buy standardised future derivatives in the forex market for hedging or speculating.

As for the commodity market, it doesn't require a separate discussion since we already discussed it at the start of the derivative section (Farmer-trader forward contracts). Just like equity, commodities are traded on exchanges. Derivatives of commodities are also traded to hedge risks or even for speculation. With this, we come to the end of our journey on financial markets. The interesting part here is that this end is your beginning. A beginning to understanding how money grows by changing hands. It shows the capital redistribution where capital moves from those who have to those who need. Knowing about the financial market is not just important for making personal financial and investment decisions, it also helps us understand the economy and world in a better way. We learned how businesses, companies, and investors make returns, protect themselves from various risks. By now, you are more than you were before you began this chapter. Let us brace ourselves for the climax chapter, where we will discuss the macro-aspects of the economy.

[1] Luthi, S. (2023, May 11). *Saving vs. investing: Understanding the key differences.*

[2] Reserve Bank of Australia. (n.d.). *The Global Financial Crisis*

# The Macro Climax: Flows and Cycles

In the last two chapters, we discussed how money moves from one hand to another in the banking and financial world. Now, it's time to take this flow to the 'economy' level. One of the fundamental principles underlying the economy is the circular flow of income. Just as the rivers never stop flowing through the streams, blood keeps moving through the veins, and air keeps blowing over the sky, money keeps flowing through the economy. With the flow of money, there is a simultaneous flow of goods and services. An economy is divided into four sectors: household, business, government, and external sector. Labour is exchanged for wages, land is exchanged for rent, capital is exchanged for interest, and entrepreneurship is exchanged for profit. This flow is a continuous loop. But there has to be a starting point or an end point from where money enters or leaves, right? Yes, the entry points are injections or inflows of money that boost economic activities. Government spending, investments by businesses or households, and the export of goods and services create an inflow of money into the economy. Activities like saving, taxes, and imports take the money out of the economy. Such outflows are often referred to as leakages.

Whenever injections are greater than leakages, there is economic expansion, while in cases when leakages become greater than injections, there is economic slowdown. Whatever the case may be, the circular flow of income never stops. It's like *Bunny* from the movie *Yeh Jawani Hai Deewani*.

Remember when Ranbir Kapoor's character *Bunny* told *Naina* (played by Deepika Padukone) what he wants in life: To rise, to fall, but never wants to stop. The circular flow of income is like this. The flow velocity may slow down or speed fast, but won't stop. How do we measure this flow of income, then? The flow is generally measured by the amount of goods and services produced in the economy. The most popular metric used is the Gross Domestic Product (GDP). One of the ways to calculate the GDP is the Expenditure Approach, where we add the expenditures incurred by individuals like you and me (denoted by C), government (denoted by G), investment by businesses (denoted by I), and Export minus the import value (X-M) [GDP = C+G+I+X-M]. The second method is called the Income Approach, where we take the sum of wage+rent+interest+profit. The third method is called the Production Approach, where we add the total output. All three methods theoretically yield the same results. What you see in the news headlines about GDP as some percentage value, like 6% or 7%, is the GDP growth rate, i.e., how much the total production value of goods and services has changed over a period of time, say, a quarter or a year.

## *The Multiplier Effect*

There are situations where we see how one event leads to another and another, and so on, thereby creating a chain reaction. We discussed the concept of money multiplier in the 4th chapter, on how initial deposits in the banking system can lead to a larger increase in the overall money supply in the economy through credit creation. Multiplier effect, on the other hand, is a broader economic concept that explains how injections of money into the economy can create a ripple effect and magnify the overall economic growth. Let's say that the government spends money to construct a highway. It also gives incentives to businesses to set up manufacturing plants and factories. When private firms invest money to set up factories, they will generate job opportunities for labourers. People from different cities might even migrate to such places for job opportunities. When factories are set up, workers will have to stay nearby, thereby boosting the real estate sector. They will demand access to various services like education, medical facilities, and recreational activities. All these will create new job opportunities, which will benefit the local population. When they start earning better, they will further add to the demand and consumption of goods and services in the economy. Better education and health of the people and their children would mean better productivity. The next generation would be better skilled. This would mean more economic activity. Better road connectivity because of highway construction would mean rapid transportation and lower logistics costs. So you see how money injected in the form of government spending and investments from private players created a virtuous cycle of prosperity.

On the contrary, if there are leakages within the economic systems, the multiplier effect weakens. What if people save all the money they earn instead of spending it on any economic activity? Savings without investments take the money out of the economy. This means that such money is not contributing to any productive activities. Neither is it generating a return through investments, nor is it creating demand for goods or services. This, however, doesn't mean we shouldn't save money. Savings for unforeseen situations and emergencies are very important. The money kept in our banks is our savings. We don't invest or spend all the money we get from our salaries, right? We even keep some money in the form of cash so that, in situations where we cannot access our bank account money, like failure of online payment or out-of-order ATMs in remote areas. What is important here is to balance our spending and savings. Being too skewed on either side can be undesirable. Similarly, imports are another category of leakage for the economy. Whenever we buy from foreign countries, money goes out of the economy as payments for such purchases. For the economy to grow, its exports must be more than its imports. This ensures that whatever money went out of the economy is compensated by a greater amount of money coming into the economy by exporting goods and services to other countries.

Then come the taxes that the government charges us. The higher the taxes, the less our disposable income (income left after paying taxes). This, in turn, means less demand in the economy. Here also, we need to remember that taxes are not bad if the government spends them judiciously. Taxes allow the government to enable the redistribution of resources that might be concentrated in just a few hands. The role of the government is to provide everyone with basic services and opportunities, and for this, they need money. So many students who cannot afford to study in schools get access to education through government schools, which are almost free of cost. If tax collection is good, then why is it considered a leakage in the economy? Theoretically, taxes are always considered a leakage in the circular flow of income because they lead to a reduction in the disposable income of people. However, in the longer run, whether taxes remain a leakage or turn into an injection depends on how the government spends them. We will come to this in a bit, but before peeping into the government's pocket, let's see exactly how the magic of the multiplier effect magnifies the injections in the economy.

## Consumer Spending and Savings: The Propensity Concept

By now, we know that savings are an important part of our financial decisions. Everyone who earns generally spends a larger proportion of their income while keeping some money aside for various goals. Some people are spendthrifts, living beyond their means, while some are miser, always saving, living a frugal life. Taking an aggregate data of people's inclinations to spend and save, we will get what is referred to as, in economics, the propensity to consume and propensity to save. On every additional increase in the income of people, the proportion of money spent gives us what is called the Marginal Propensity to Consume (MPC), while the proportion of savings on every additional income is the Marginal Propensity to Save (MPS). Taking on the previous example where the government injected money to construct a highway, let's assume that the budget for highway construction was ₹100 crores. This government expenditure of ₹100 crores creates initial income worth ₹100 crores for workers, suppliers, and other entities involved in the highway construction. Out of this additional income, let us assume that people spend ₹80 crores while saving ₹20 crores. The formula to calculate MPC and MPS is Change in consumption/Change in Income and Change in Savings/Change in Income, respectively. Therefore, here, the MPC would be 0.8 (80/100) and the MPS would be 0.2 (20/100). Since every additional income would either be spent or saved, the sum of MPC and MPS would always be equal to 1.

Here, due to the initial injection of ₹100 crores, people created additional demand in the economy by spending ₹80 crores. This ₹80 crores again acted as an injection in the economy due to demand creation, just like the previous injection of ₹100 crores. Since the share of spending and savings is 80% and 20%, respectively, people would spend ₹64 crores (80% of 80 crores), saving ₹16 crores. Now, this ₹64 crores has again turned into an injection in the economy, out of which ₹51.2 crores (80% of 64 crores) will be spent, and the rest saved. This chain will continue for several rounds. Adding all the injections would give us the total income generated in the economy. To ease this calculation, we have a simple formula to get to the final numbers, and that is, Multiplier = 1/1-MPC, which can also be written as 1/MPS. Using this formula, we get the multiplier value as 5 (1/1-0.8 or 1/0.2). This means an initial injection of ₹100 crore through government spending will ultimately generate ₹500 crore of total GDP over several rounds (5*100 crores). The higher the propensity to consume, the stronger the multiplier effect. This is because when more income is spent, the money that gets recirculated in the economy is higher. This kind of spending, which happens because people earn more money, is what keeps the cycle going - spending leads to income, and income leads to more spending. If the spending vs saving share had been 50-50, then the multiplier value would have been 2 (1/0.5), generating only ₹200 crore from an initial injection of ₹100 crore. Understanding the multiplier effect becomes important, especially for the government, which plays a vital role in the initial injection levels. The government makes policies to stimulate economic growth. Such polices are referred to as fiscal policy. In the last section, we left off at our discussion about the nature of government expenditure. Let us come back to that now.

## Government Budget: Revenue and Capital Side

The government's budget, meaning the financial planning of the government, has two parts. One part is the government expenditure. This, too, is further classified into two types: revenue expenditure and capital expenditure. All those expenses that are routine in nature, like giving salaries, pensions, and administrative costs, come under revenue expenditure. Such expenditure neither creates any asset nor changes any liability for the government. Giving certain financial benefits or support to a certain section of the economy, like providing goods or services, free of cost or at a discounted price, or providing tax concessions or even direct cash payments by the government, is called a subsidy. The government may give subsidies for various reasons. For example, the government can distribute free sewing machines to rural women. This would enable them to start earning through tailoring. However, at times, such free distribution may not create any positive impact on the economy. For instance, cash distribution to people might lead to them ending up spending on bad things like liquor or gambling. Such activity doesn't create any long-lasting positive impact on the economy. Neither does it create any new job opportunities, nor does it improve the productivity of people. Therefore, revenue expenditure like this can be a drain on the economy. It's important to recognize that not all revenue expenditures are harmful. Many are essential for the smooth functioning of administration and play a crucial role in redistributing wealth to reduce economic inequality. However, distinguishing between beneficial and harmful subsidies can be a complex challenge. The political and media debates around the "freebies" culture need the attention of policymakers so that we can have a consensus on which types of subsidies may be considered appropriate for the welfare of our society and which ones would put a strain on the public finances[1].

Capital expenditure, on the other hand, is that which creates assets or changes the liabilities for the government. Government spending on highway construction, schools, and hospitals, opening skill training centers for youth, is all part of the capital expenditure and has positive effects on the economy. Such expenses will boost economic productivity. In the 5th chapter, we read how the government raises debt through various means, like the issuance of government securities or bonds. Such borrowings need to be repaid. Such repayment of loans also forms a part of the capital expenditure because these expenses are reducing the government liabilities (loans are the liability for borrowers and an asset for the lenders). To sum up, if the tax money is spent more on asset building, it's good for the economy, while if it is spent too much on subsidies and free goods as a vote bank politics (to attract votes from the electors), it can put strain on the public finances.

Now that we have seen what goes out of the government's purse, let's also glance through what comes into the purse to get a clear picture of the whole budget. The money that the government receives is called receipt. Just like the two types of expenditure, receipts are also of two types, revenue receipts and capital receipts. Any money coming to the government without creating any asset or liability falls under revenue receipt. All the taxes, direct, indirect, fees, fines, charges, collected by the government are revenue receipts since they are neither creating assets nor liabilities that need to be repaid. On the other hand, if the government sells its factory, or some company (government-owned companies are called Public Sector Undertakings, or PSUs), whole or some portion, it would be a part of capital receipt. This is because such a sale of ownership reduces the government's assets. Selling some stakes (equity) of its PSUs to private players is called disinvesment. Disinvestment is different from privatisation. In privatisation, the government sells the majority of its ownership (51% or more) to private players, while in disinvestment, the majority ownership is still with the government (over 50%). Contrary to disinvestment and privatisation, if the government takes over the majority stakes of any private company, becoming a majority shareholder, it's called nationalisation. For instance, the Government of India, in 1969, nationalised 14 private banks. Now that we have discussed what is what, can you tell what type of receipts the government borrowings are? If your answer is: Capital receipt, you can give yourself 10 points, for you are now clear with the government budget.

If we take the case of India, we follow a balanced budget. This means that the receipt side is equal to the expenditure side. Does that mean the government spends 100% of what it earns? In our households, we must have seen our parents spend 80-90% of their incomes while saving the rest. It also happens when, in some months, they spend 100% of what they earn. Does the government also do the same? To your surprise, the government often spends more than what it earns (Over 100% of its income). We know that taxes and disinvestment or sale of their assets form the earnings of the government. So, if the government collected, say, ₹60 crores from all forms of taxes and received ₹40 crores from the sale of its ownership, giving a total income of ₹100 crores, will the government's expense be equal to ₹100 crores? No! The government could be spending, say, ₹120 crores. Where did this extra ₹20 crore come from? This ₹20 crore is the money borrowed by the government and is the deficit amount. The difference between the government expenditure and income is thus called the fiscal deficit. Here, ₹20 crore is the amount of fiscal deficit for the government that needs to be repaid to the lenders. A high fiscal deficit means fewer injections in the future due to the repayment burden on future dates. However, some amount of fiscal deficit can prove to be good for the economy if the borrowed money is used for investment purposes by the government. For example, the government can increase its spending on Research and Development (R&D). Higher innovations would lead to greater productivity, more employment opportunities. When employment levels increase, the tax base would also increase. This means higher tax collections by the government, and thus, the money borrowed by the government can easily be repaid. If, on the other hand, the government uses the borrowed money on revenue receipts, that doesn't create any asset; it would lead to a negative spiral, ultimately putting further pressure on the government's finances. The positive and negative spiral is discussed in the next section in greater detail.

## The Cycle of Virtue and Vice

Depending on the levels of injections and leakages, a self-reinforcing loop gets created. The positive one is called a virtuous cycle, while the negative one is called a vicious cycle. Whenever there are high levels of investments in the economy, it creates more opportunities. Investments improve the overall productivity, thereby leading to more job creation. Higher employment level means higher aggregate income levels in the economy. When people earn more, they will spend more. Higher consumer demand pushes businesses to increase their production levels to match the demand. This, in turn, leads to further investment, thereby creating a virtuous loop of more investment leading to more investment. Vicious cycles are just the opposite. Poor economic growth leads to lower profit levels for businesses. This pushes the businesses to cut down on their cost by laying off (firing workers) and lowering production. Lower employment levels mean less income with the people. This would mean less consumer demand in the economy. When businesses see less demand, they lower their production even further, creating a negative loop. To break such a vicious cycle, the government needs to intervene in the form of stimulus packages, like those given during the COVID-19 pandemic by governments of many economies. Such a stimulus package involves incentives for boosting consumer demand in the economy. The government also provides tax reliefs to people to enhance their level of disposable income. Such measures form a part of the fiscal policy. Central banks of the economies, too, play a role in breaking out of the vicious cycles through their monetary policy measures. To boost consumer demand, they lower the policy rates, thereby making bank loans cheaper to access (due to lower interest rates). If sluggish economic growth stems from structural issues, the government must implement reforms focused on boosting labor productivity, enhancing skill development, improving youth nutrition, and increasing female workforce participation.

## Externalities: The Unnoticed, The Unaccountable

The positives and negatives of an economy are not just limited to what is visible in the form of economic growth or slowdown. There are invisible areas as well, which often go unnoticed. This is because the impact of such positives and negatives is indirect and affects third parties. Such impacts are termed as externalities: Positive and Negative. Positive externalities are the external benefits received by those not directly involved in a transaction. For example, a pharmaceutical company achieved a breakthrough in its research work on a vaccine. This benefited the company directly by getting their work patented, allowing them to make profits from its sale. The external benefits are for those people suffering from a disease against which the vaccine was developed. An organisation established a school to educate girls. The direct beneficiaries were the girls who got educated from the school, leading to them getting employment opportunities. The positive externality involved here is the lower crime levels in the society since those educated girls, upon their marriage, would teach their children good habits, making them responsible citizens who abide by the laws of the land.

Negative externalities, on the other hand, refer to the external costs, or the negative impact on those not directly involved. For instance, factories manufacturing some goods discharge the untreated wastewater into the river bodies. This would affect the marine species, like the fish. A lower fish population would mean higher chances of losses for the fishermen. Fishes thriving in such polluted water would lead to the transfer of harmful effects to the humans consuming them. This, in biology, is called biomagnification. So you see how negative externalities are a problem. What's the solution, then? As the economies grow, it becomes more and more complex. Things don't remain black and white. To address the grey areas, we need better regulations, collaboration, and stakeholder consultations to resolve such issues. The negative externality of industrialisation or urbanisation is evident in the form of climate change. Rapid economic growth might be giving us higher GDP numbers, but the externality here is the strain it is putting on the natural resources and our environment. We cannot afford to neglect them. Today, some of the most developed cities are the ones where the air is the most polluted. Instances of flash floods in urban areas have become so common. Too much concretisation of cities has led to the shrinkage of green land[2]. Development in one country has a negative externality for another country. It's not the rich countries that are suffering the most from climate change. It's the people from the least developed countries, where drought, floods, and submerging coastal areas due to rising sea levels have forced the local people to migrate[3].

Only when we recognise the externalities, we will be able to encourage and incentivize activities with positive externalities and discourage those with negative ones. Balancing growth and environmental sustainability is important. Such balancing requires not just domestic efforts but also international collaborations. Recognizing the negative externalities of unsustainable economic growth, governments and organizations have started pushing for green finance. Many governments and organisations are raising money through the issuance of green bonds. The money raised through such bonds would be used to finance environmentally sustainable projects. A subset of green bonds is the blue bonds. They are particularly for protecting and conserving the marine ecosystem. Likewise, carbon markets have emerged to mitigate carbon emissions and incentivize businesses to reduce their carbon footprints. Since carbon emissions contribute to global warming, many countries have put a cap on the amount of emissions businesses can emit. Many companies, through investment in renewable energy and innovation, have lowered their carbon emissions below the set limits, while many haven't. With every unit of lower emissions achieved, carbon credits are created, which can be traded in the carbon market. To offset their emissions levels, companies and businesses can voluntarily purchase these carbon credits. This mechanism is called the cap-and-trade system. Climate change is the result of unsustainable economic growth. To mitigate climate change, we cannot let economic growth be hampered. Do you know what happens when the economic growth slows down? Let's find out in the next section.

## Boom and Bust: The Economic Cycle

Economic growth happens in cycles. A cycle, again? Yes, such growth cycles are also called business cycles, and they involve periods of expansion and contraction. If you visualize this on a graph sheet, it would look like a wave. The phase corresponding to the upward graph line is called the boom, while the downward graph line represents the phase of bust. Graphs are plotted based on the change in GDP rates. The downward phase, or the bust, is also called a recession. During recessions, there is a widespread decline in economic activity. A common metric to tell if the economy is going through a recession is to check the GDP rates over two quarters (a financial year is divided into four quarters). If the GDP declines for two consecutive quarters, it is widely considered a recession. The 2008 financial crisis brought a recession across many countries, starting with the USA. The world faced a recessionary phase even during the COVID-19 pandemic, causing lockdowns across many countries. Boom and bust are therefore the outcome of the virtuous and vicious cycles we just discussed. It's also important to note that these two are not the same. It's the latter ones that cause the former, respectively. The business cycle is not a uniform wave of periodic expansion and contraction. They can be erratic depending on many factors. They don't follow a predictable pattern.

## *Predicting Recessions: The Yield Curve Way*

We discussed the bond market in great depth in the 5th chapter. Now we know that bond yield refers to the return on the bond investment as a percentage. If you can recall, we discussed the difference between interest rate and yield rate. Since the bond price keeps changing in the secondary market, due to changes in its demand, the yield rates also keep changing. Bonds come with different maturity periods, like 1-year, 3-year, 5-year, 10-year, 30-year, or even 50-year, depending on the needs of the bond issuer. The yield curve is a graph where we plot the yields of different maturity bonds. Visualize a graph with the x-axis representing the time of bond maturity and the y-axis representing the yield. When we join all the plots, we get an upward slope indicating that higher-maturity bonds give greater yields. The logic behind this trend is that investors demand higher yields on long-term bonds because such bonds carry higher risks. We know that over the years, inflation would erode the value of the money. Also, since investors' money would get locked for a longer duration, they expect a higher return as a reward for investing in such bonds. Finally, no one knows what's going to happen in the future. We can analyse things for the near term, but predicting the long-term future is very difficult. What would be the economic and financial conditions during the maturity of such bonds? What if the issuer of the bonds defaults? Such unpredictability demands a higher return on their investments. All these factors lead to an upward sloping yield curve.

Now that we know what a yield curve is and what it looks like, in a usual situation, let's get to the unusual part. There are instances when the yield curve becomes inverted, meaning the upward sloping curve changes to a downward sloping curve. Why does this happen? Downward slope would mean that the yields on longer-maturity bonds are less than the yields on shorter-maturity ones. The reason is simple: Demand and supply mismatch. When demand for longer maturity bonds increases, more than for shorter-maturity bonds, the yield curve inverts. Experts generally use the yield curve to predict economic cycles, specifically, recessions. Such observations are concerning the government bonds. The most common trend for a recessionary signal is the difference between the 3-month and 10-year yield for the US market. When the 3-month yield exceeds the 10-year yield, experts start predicting a potential recession in the economy. Generally, investors keep a sense of how the market is performing, what the potential risks and returns are on different investment options. Whenever investors sense a potential recession in the near term, they rush towards buying long-term bonds as safer investment options. This increase in demand for long-term bonds increases their price, thereby causing a decline in their yields. Meanwhile, the shorter tenure bonds remain high due to the central bank's policy stances. We read in the 3<sup>rd</sup> chapter, that to curb inflation, central banks issue higher interest rate bonds to suck in the liquidity from the economy. Such moves, in extreme cases, may lead to lower economic production, thereby creating fear among investors of a potential recession. Thus, they flock towards longer maturity bonds. So, this is the whole story of the inverted yield curve and how it gives us early warning signals of a recession[4]. It signals an economic slowdown and is not a guarantee of recession, since other factors, too, contribute to a recession or no recession.

Everything we have discussed in this book so far has the potential to affect the business cycles of economies. From demand and supply levels in the economy to price and inflation levels, to interest rates in the banking system, to trade patterns in financial markets, to positive and negative externalities, all are potential factors for boosting or contracting economic activities. When the overall economic activity slows down, consumption goes down, which induces cuts in production levels, and the cycle continues. Fiscal and monetary interventions by the government and central banks of economies have the power to change the trend of the cycle. Governments generally follow a type of fiscal policy called Counter-cyclical Fiscal Policy. Under this, they take measures that aim to reverse the flow of income, and make it go in the opposite direction to the existing business cycle. During a recession, when the flow of income is slow, the government would lower taxes and increase its spending to boost the flow of income in the economy, while during a boom, it would lower its spending and hike taxes to control the flow of income, so as to avoid overstimulation, leading to high inflation levels. Finally, business cycles are not just driven by economic policies, interest rates, or market forces. There's another very important aspect which we haven't touched yet.

## Humanizing Economics: A Full Circle

Human psychology is often an overlooked aspect of economic cycles. Public sentiments, human emotions of fear, greed, herd mentality, optimism, and sometimes, even over-optimism have played roles during boom and bust. After all, whatever we have discussed up until now is based on the way we behave or react, or deal with things under different circumstances. All those MPC and MPS are coming from the human behavioral aspects. The part of economics where we study and analyze human behavior is called behavioral economics. Let me share an instance with you. While writing this very chapter of the book, there was a new trend on social media: people turning their selfies and pictures into Ghibli-style AI-generated images. Every other person on social media was posting such images. The source of the image generation was an AI chatbot whose CEO had to put a limit on the number of images that could be generated per user because the trend had put so much pressure on their processing software (Graphics Processing Units, or GPUs). Such herd mentality and FOMO (Fear Of Missing Out) created by social media have given rise to a whole new economy of attention. Remember, we discussed this in the very first chapter. Reels, podcasts, and trends have shaped the way marketing departments of companies work.

An interesting theory of human psychology is the hedonic adaptation. This aspect of human psychology has given rise to trends like shopping hauls, "unboxing" videos, and GRWM (Get Ready With Me). Hedonic adaptation theory states that humans tend to return to a stable level of happiness after experiencing negative or positive emotions[5]. Whenever we buy a new item, don't we feel excited for some duration? The excitement could last for a few months, a few days, or even a few hours. Once the euphoria subsides, we start craving more. On watching content like unboxing expensive gadgets or shopping hauls by content creators, or celebrities getting ready videos, many people end up over-buying and overspending[6]. This is evident from the rise in the number of make-up and clothing brands emerging in recent times. Influencer marketing, higher purchasing power, and easy access to the latest fashion trends have given rise to the fast fashion industry[7]. Many people who can't even afford expensive stuff own them through features like Buy-Now-Pay-Later available on online payment platforms[8]. This has given a boost to the fintech sector, which is collaborating with traditional banks to provide easy credit. So you see how human psychology plays a role in giving a boost to so many industries[9].

A large part of the financial market thrives on human psychology. When investors become too greedy or over-optimistic about a sector, it can create a bubble by artificially inflating the prices. The 2008 financial crisis is one of the most evident examples of this. Most people believed that housing prices would never fall and so kept on investing and speculating. At times, the reverse happens. People start to panic seeing some market correction (a fall in stock prices to reach their actual worth). Such panic happens even in the banking system, where panic creeps in and everyone starts taking out their deposits from banks, a situation called a bank run. There's a fallacy found in human behaviour called loss aversion. People fear losses more than they enjoy gains. Such a bias among people pushes them to hold on to certain investments, even after going into a loss, in the hope of their recovery[10]. Advertisers use such fallacies in their favour by framing their ads in a way that makes the consumers feel the fear of missing out. Taglines like "Limited Edition", Hurry Up! Few tickets left" creates an illusion of urgency and scarcity among people. They know that humans fear losing out on something, and so they market their products that way. Understanding human psychology is not just helpful for businesses to market their product; it's also important for us as individuals to know how and why we behave the way we do. This will not just help us in making better decisions for our finances (investments and spending), but it will also make us aware of how the whole economic system works. Having a broader perspective always gives us an edge.

We started this book from the decision-making aspect of ours in the form of opportunity cost, and now, we conclude this book with human behavior. Not just this chapter, but the whole book has come full circle. On this note, we end our conversation here. Hope you enjoyed this short journey. I also hope that this will be your start of another journey of learning economics and finance in greater depth.

[1] Reuters. (2025). *India's top court says handouts creating 'class of parasites', Live Law reports.*

[2] NASA. (2023). *Urbanization and Flash Floods: How Cities Affect Rainfall.*

[3] UNFCCC. (2023). *Loss and Damage: Addressing the Harms of Climate Change.*

[4] Federal Reserve Bank of St. Louis. (2023). *The Yield Curve and Recession Predictability.*

[5] Brickman, P., & Campbell, D. T. (1971). *Hedonic Relativism and Planning the Good Society. Adaptation-Level Theory,* 287-305.

[6] Alter, A. (2017). *Irresistible: The Rise of Addictive Technology and the Business of Keeping Us Hooked.* Penguin Press.

[7] McKinsey & Company. (2023). *Fast Fashion: Trends and Consumer Behavior.*

[8] World Economic Forum. (2022). *The Rise of Buy Now, Pay Later: A Behavioral Economic Perspective.*

[9] Akerlof, G. A., & Shiller, R. J. (2010). *Animal Spirits: How Human Psychology Drives the Economy, and Why It Matters for Global Capitalism.* Princeton University Press

[10] Tversky, A., & Kahneman, D. (1991). *Loss Aversion in Riskless Choice: A Reference-Dependent Model. The Quarterly Journal of Economics, 106*(4), 1039-1061.

# Further Reading


**Chapter 1:**
  **Fundamental Economic Concepts**

- Mankiw, N. G. (2020). *Principles of Economics* (9th ed.). Cengage Learning.
- Samuelson, P. A., & Nordhaus, W. D. (2010). *Economics* (19th ed.). McGraw-Hill Education.
- Krugman, P., & Wells, R. (2021). *Microeconomics* (6th ed.). Worth Publishers.

**Decision-Making & Opportunity Cost**

- Thaler, R. H. (2015). *Misbehaving: The Making of Behavioral Economics*. W.W. Norton & Company.
- Kahneman, D. (2011). *Thinking, Fast and Slow*. Farrar, Straus and Giroux.
- Becker, G. S. (1976). *The Economic Approach to Human Behavior*. University of Chicago Press.

**Rational Choice & Efficiency**

- Buchanan, J. M. (1979). *What Should Economists Do?* Liberty Fund.
- Varian, H. R. (2014). *Intermediate Microeconomics: A Modern Approach* (9th ed.). W.W. Norton & Company.
- Kaldor, N. (1939). Welfare propositions in economics and interpersonal comparisons of utility. *The Economic Journal, 49*(195), 549-552.

**Trade-Offs, Government Decisions & Policy**

- Stiglitz, J. E. (2000). *Economics of the Public Sector* (3rd ed.).

W.W. Norton & Company.
- Musgrave, R. A., & Musgrave, P. B. (1989). *Public Finance in Theory and Practice.* McGraw-Hill Education.
- Ricardo, D. (1817). *On the Principles of Political Economy and Taxation.* John Murray.

## Opportunity Cost in Business & Finance

- Brealey, R. A., Myers, S. C., & Allen, F. (2020). *Principles of Corporate Finance* (13th ed.). McGraw-Hill Education.
- Friedman, M. (1962). *Capitalism and Freedom.* University of Chicago Press.
- Drucker, P. (2006). *The Effective Executive: The Definitive Guide to Getting the Right Things Done.* HarperBusiness.

## Behavioral Economics & Attention as a Resource

- Simon, H. A. (1971). Designing organizations for an information-rich world. *Computers, Communications, and the Public Interest,* 40(1), 37-52.
- Goldhaber, M. H. (1997). The attention economy and the Net. *First Monday,* 2(4).
- Wu, T. (2016). *The Attention Merchants: The Epic Scramble to Get Inside Our Heads.* Knopf.

## Social & Psychological Impacts of Opportunity Cost
*Rebellious, More Tolerant, Less Happy—and Completely Unprepared for Adulthood.* Atria Books.

## Resource Scarcity, Innovation & Jevons Paradox

- Jevons, W. S. (1865). *The Coal Question: An Inquiry Concerning the Progress of the*
- Schwartz, B. (2004). *The Paradox of Choice: Why More Is Less.* Harper Perennial.
- Ariely, D. (2008). *Predictably Irrational: The Hidden Forces That*

*Shape Our Decisions*. HarperCollins.
- Twenge, J. M. (2017). *iGen: Why Today's Super-Connected Kids Are Growing Up Less*
- *Nation, and the Probable Exhaustion of Our Coal Mines.* Macmillan and Co.
- Hardin, G. (1968). The tragedy of the commons. *Science, 162*(3859), 1243-1248.
- Ellen MacArthur Foundation. (2013). *Towards the Circular Economy: Economic and Business Rationale for an Accelerated Transition.*

### Chapter 2:
### Demand & Supply Concepts

- Mankiw, N. G. (2020). *Principles of Economics* (9th ed.). Cengage Learning.
- Krugman, P., & Wells, R. (2018). *Microeconomics* (5th ed.). Worth Publishers.

### Definition & Law of Demand

- Marshall, A. (1890). *Principles of Economics*. Macmillan.
- Samuelson, P. A., & Nordhaus, W. D. (2010). *Economics* (19th ed.). McGraw-Hill.

### Utility Concept & Utility Maximization

- Jevons, W. S. (1871). *The Theory of Political Economy*. Macmillan.
- Edgeworth, F. Y. (1881). *Mathematical Psychics: An Essay on the Application of Mathematics to the Moral Sciences*. Kegan Paul.

### Definition & Law of Supply

- Stigler, G. J. (1946). *The Theory of Price*. Macmillan.

### Logic Behind the Law of Demand & Supply

- Hicks, J. R. (1939). *Value and Capital: An Inquiry into Some Fundamental Principles of Economic Theory*. Oxford University Press.
- Becker, G. S. (1976). *The Economic Approach to Human Behavior*. University of Chicago Press.

### Exceptions to the Law of Demand (Veblen Goods, Giffen Goods, Substitution Effect)

- Veblen, T. (1899). *The Theory of the Leisure Class*. Macmillan.
- Giffen, R. (1890). *A Paradox in Economics: The Case of Giffen Goods*. Economic Journal, 1(2), 15-23.
- Slutsky, E. (1915). *On the Theory of the Budget of the Consumer*. Giornale Degli Economisti.

### Exceptions to the Law of Supply

- Kaldor, N. (1934). *A Classificatory Note on the Determinateness of Equilibrium. The Review of Economic Studies*, 1(2), 122-136.
- Stiglitz, J. E. (1987). *Competition and the Number of Firms in a Market: Are Duopolies More Competitive than Atomistic Markets?* Journal of Political Economy, 95(5), 1041-1061.

### Market Equilibrium Concept

- Walras, L. (1874). *Elements of Pure Economics*. Lausanne.
- Arrow, K. J., & Debreu, G. (1954). *Existence of an Equilibrium for a Competitive Economy*. Econometrica, 22(3), 265-290.

### Concept of Price Elasticity & Inelasticity

- Marshall, A. (1890). *Principles of Economics*. Macmillan.
- Lerner, A. P. (1933). *The Concept of Monopoly and the*

*Measurement of Monopoly Power.* Review of Economic Studies, *1*(3), 157-175.

## Chapter 3:
## Definition & Concept of Inflation

- Mankiw, N. G. (2020). *Principles of Economics* (9th ed.). Cengage Learning.
- Samuelson, P. A., & Nordhaus, W. D. (2010). *Economics* (19th ed.). McGraw-Hill.

### Measuring Inflation (CPI, WPI, etc.)

- Mishkin, F. S. (2019). *The Economics of Money, Banking, and Financial Markets* (13th ed.). Pearson.
- Dornbusch, R., Fischer, S., & Startz, R. (2013). *Macroeconomics* (12th ed.). McGraw-Hill.

### Measuring Inflation in India

- Reserve Bank of India. (n.d.). *Monetary Policy Framework.* Available at: https://www.rbi.org.in
- Ministry of Statistics and Programme Implementation (MoSPI), Government of India. (n.d.). *Consumer Price Index (CPI) & Wholesale Price Index (WPI) Reports.*

### Case Study: Hyperinflation in Zimbabwe

- Hanke, S. H., & Kwok, A. K. F. (2009). *On the Measurement of Zimbabwe's Hyperinflation.* Cato Journal, *29*(2), 353-364.
- IMF. (2008). *Zimbabwe: Challenges and Policy Options after Hyperinflation.* Available at: https://www.imf.org

### Economics Behind Inflation

- Keynes, J. M. (1936). *The General Theory of Employment, Interest, and Money.* Macmillan.
- Blanchard, O. (2017). *Macroeconomics* (7th ed.). Pearson.

**Milton Friedman's Monetarist Theory on Inflation**

- Friedman, M. (1968). *The Role of Monetary Policy.* American Economic Review, *58*(1), 1-17.
- Friedman, M., & Schwartz, A. J. (1963). *A Monetary History of the United States, 1867-1960.* Princeton University Press.

**Government Stimulus Packages During COVID-19 & Inflation**

- International Monetary Fund. (2021). *World Economic Outlook: Inflation and Policy Response Post-COVID.* Available at: https://www.imf.org
- Reserve Bank of India. (2020). *RBI's Response to COVID-19: Liquidity Measures & Inflation Impact.* Available at: https://www.rbi.org.in

**Structuralist Theory of Inflation**

- Taylor, L. (1983). *Structuralist Macroeconomics: Applicable Models for the Third World.* Basic Books.
- Bresser-Pereira, L. C., & Nakano, Y. (1987). *The Theory of Inertial Inflation: The Foundation of Economic Reform in Brazil & Argentina.* World Development, *15*(3), 351-365.

**Network Effect as a Cause of Inflation**

- Shapiro, C., & Varian, H. R. (1998). *Information Rules: A Strategic Guide to the Network Economy.* Harvard Business Press.
- Katz, M. L., & Shapiro, C. (1985). *Network Externalities, Competition, and Compatibility.* American Economic Review,

*75*(3), 424-440.

## Is Inflation Always Bad? Positives of Inflation


- Tobin, J. (1972). *Inflation and Unemployment*. American Economic Review, *62*(1), 1-18.
- Akerlof, G. A., Dickens, W. T., & Perry, G. L. (1996). *The Macroeconomics of Low Inflation*. Brookings Papers on Economic Activity, *1996*(1), 1-59.


## Why Some Level of Inflation is Needed in the Economy


- Summers, L. H. (1991). *How Should Long-Term Monetary Policy Be Determined?*. Journal of Money, Credit, and Banking, *23*(3), 625-631.


## Who Benefits & Who Suffers from Inflation?


- Piketty, T. (2014). *Capital in the Twenty-First Century*. Harvard University Press.
- Stiglitz, J. E. (2012). *The Price of Inequality: How Today's Divided Society Endangers Our Future*. W.W. Norton & Company.


## Policies to Deal with Inflation


- Mishkin, F. S. (2019). *The Economics of Money, Banking, and Financial Markets* (13th ed.). Pearson.
- Bernanke, B. S. (2007). *Inflation Expectations and Inflation Policy*. Speech at the National Bureau of Economic Research.


## Monetary & Fiscal Policy Measures to Deal with Inflation


- Blinder, A. S. (1982). *Issues in the Coordination of Monetary and Fiscal Policy*. National Bureau of Economic Research.
- Barro, R. J. (1979). *On the Determination of Public Debt*. Journal

of Political Economy, *87*(5), 940-971.

## How Inflation is Tackled in India

- Reserve Bank of India. (2022). *Monetary Policy Report*. Available at: https://www.rbi.org.in
- Government of India. (2021). *Union Budget Reports: Fiscal Policies & Inflation Management*. Available at: https://www.indiabudget.gov.in

## RBI's Monetary Policy Tools to Deal with Inflation

- Reserve Bank of India. (2020). *Monetary Policy Framework and Inflation Targeting in India*. Available at: https://www.rbi.org.in
- Patra, M. D. (2021). *Monetary Policy in India: Framework and Instruments*. Speech at the International Monetary Fund.

## Types of Inflation

- **Demand-Pull Inflation**

  - Keynes, J. M. (1936). *The General Theory of Employment, Interest, and Money*. Macmillan.
  - Mankiw, N. G. (2020). *Macroeconomics* (10th ed.). Worth Publishers.

- **Cost-Push Inflation**

  - Samuelson, P. A., & Nordhaus, W. D. (2010). *Economics* (19th ed.). McGraw-Hill.
  - Dornbusch, R., Fischer, S., & Startz, R. (2013). *Macroeconomics* (12th ed.). McGraw-Hill.

- **Built-In (Wage-Price Spiral) Inflation**

- Blanchard, O. (2017). *Macroeconomics* (7th ed.). Pearson.
- Tobin, J. (1972). *Inflation and Unemployment*. American Economic Review, 62(1), 1-18.

- **Hyperinflation**

  - Hanke, S. H., & Kwok, A. K. F. (2009). *On the Measurement of Zimbabwe's Hyperinflation*. Cato Journal, 29(2), 353-364.
  - Sargent, T. J. (1982). *The Ends of Four Big Inflations*. In *Inflation: Causes and Effects* (pp. 41-97). University of Chicago Press.

- **Stagflation**

  - Phelps, E. S. (1968). *Money-Wage Dynamics and Labor Market Equilibrium*. Journal of Political Economy, 76(4), 678-711.
  - Friedman, M. (1976). *Nobel Lecture: Inflation and Unemployment*. Journal of Political Economy, 85(3), 451-472.

- **Deflation & Disinflation**

  - Fisher, I. (1933). *The Debt-Deflation Theory of Great Depressions*. Econometrica, 1(4), 337-357.
  - Bernanke, B. S. (2002). *Deflation: Making Sure "It" Doesn't Happen Here*. Speech at the National Economists Club, Washington, D.C.


## Causes of Inflation


- **Excessive Money Supply (Monetarist View)**

  - Friedman, M. (1968). *The Role of Monetary Policy*. American Economic Review, 58(1), 1-17.
  - Friedman, M., & Schwartz, A. J. (1963). *A Monetary History of the United States, 1867-1960*. Princeton University Press.

- **Demand-Pull Factors**

  - Keynes, J. M. (1936). *The General Theory of Employment, Interest, and Money*. Macmillan.
  - Mishkin, F. S. (2019). *The Economics of Money, Banking, and Financial Markets* (13th ed.). Pearson.

- **Cost-Push Factors (Supply-Side Constraints)**

  - Samuelson, P. A., & Nordhaus, W. D. (2010). *Economics* (19th ed.). McGraw-Hill.
  - Dornbusch, R., Fischer, S., & Startz, R. (2013). *Macroeconomics* (12th ed.). McGraw-Hill.

- **Wage-Price Spiral**

  - Tobin, J. (1972). *Inflation and Unemployment*. American Economic Review, 62(1), 1-18.
  - Blanchard, O. (2017). *Macroeconomics* (7th ed.). Pearson.

- **Structural Factors (Structuralist Inflation)**

  - Taylor, L. (1983). *Structuralist Macroeconomics: Applicable Models for the Third World*. Basic Books.
  - Bresser-Pereira, L. C., & Nakano, Y. (1987). *The Theory of Inertial Inflation: The Foundation of Economic Reform in Brazil & Argentina*. World Development, *15*(3), 351-365.

- **External Factors (Imported Inflation & Currency Depreciation)**

  - Dornbusch, R. (1976). *Expectations and Exchange Rate Dynamics*. Journal of Political Economy, 84(6), 1161-1176.
  - Krugman, P., & Obstfeld, M. (2022). *International Economics: Theory and Policy* (12th ed.). Pearson.

<u>Chapter 4:</u>
## History of Saving Money & Evolution of Banking

- **History of Saving Money & Piggy Banks**

  - Ferguson, N. (2008). *The Ascent of Money: A Financial History of the World.* Penguin Books.
  - Goetzmann, W. N. (2016). *Money Changes Everything: How Finance Made Civilization Possible.* Princeton University Press.

- **Evolution of Assets (Physical to Financial Instruments)**

  - Kindleberger, C. P., & Aliber, R. Z. (2011). *Manias, Panics, and Crashes: A History of Financial Crises* (6th ed.). Palgrave Macmillan.
  - Malkiel, B. G. (2019). *A Random Walk Down Wall Street: The Time-Tested Strategy for Successful Investing* (12th ed.). W. W. Norton & Company.

- **Why We Keep Money in Banks & What Are Banks?**

  - Mishkin, F. S. (2019). *The Economics of Money, Banking, and Financial Markets* (13th ed.). Pearson.
  - Fabozzi, F. J., Modigliani, F., Jones, F. J., & Ferri, M. (2014). *Foundations of Financial Markets and Institutions* (4th ed.). Pearson.

- **Evolution of Banking System & Early Banking in Venice and Florence**

  - De Roover, R. (1963). *The Rise and Decline of the Medici Bank: 1397-1494.* Harvard University Press.
  - Braudel, F. (1982). *The Wheels of Commerce* (Vol. 2). Harper & Row.

- **The Medici Bank of Florence**

  - Parks, T. (2013). *Medici Money: Banking, Metaphysics, and Art in Fifteenth-Century Florence.* W. W. Norton & Company.
  - Goldthwaite, R. A. (2015). *The Economy of Renaissance Florence.* Johns Hopkins University Press.

**Banking Concepts & Systems**

- **Fractional Reserve Banking & Money Multiplier**

  - Mishkin, F. S. (2019). *The Economics of Money, Banking, and Financial Markets* (13th ed.). Pearson.
  - Samuelson, P. A., & Nordhaus, W. D. (2010). *Economics* (19th ed.). McGraw-Hill.

- **Fractional Reserve System in Indian Banking**

  - Reserve Bank of India (2023). *Report on Trends and Progress of Banking in India.* RBI Publications.
  - Sengupta, R., & Vardhan, H. (2019). *Tracing the Evolution of the Indian Banking Sector.* Brookings India Working Paper No. 03.

- **Money Market & Money Market in India**

  - Fabozzi, F. J. (2013). *The Handbook of Fixed Income Securities* (8th ed.). McGraw-Hill.
  - Reserve Bank of India (2022). *Handbook of Statistics on the Indian Economy.* RBI.

**Banking Risks, Regulations & Crises**

- **Trust as the Foundation of the Banking System**

- Reinhart, C. M., & Rogoff, K. S. (2009). *This Time Is Different: Eight Centuries of Financial Folly.* Princeton University Press.
- Gorton, G. (2012). *Misunderstanding Financial Crises: Why We Don't See Them Coming.* Oxford University Press.


### Bank Runs: Concept & Case Studies


- Diamond, D. W., & Dybvig, P. H. (1983). *Bank Runs, Deposit Insurance, and Liquidity.* Journal of Political Economy, *91*(3), 401-419.
- Kindleberger, C. P., & Aliber, R. Z. (2011). *Manias, Panics, and Crashes: A History of Financial Crises.* Palgrave Macmillan.


### Emergence of Banking Regulations & Role of Central Banks


- Goodhart, C. A. E. (1988). *The Evolution of Central Banks.* MIT Press.
- Mishkin, F. S. (2019). *The Economics of Money, Banking, and Financial Markets* (13th ed.). Pearson.


### Role of RBI in Indian Banking System


- Chakrabarty, K. C. (2011). *Indian Banking: Regulation, Supervision, and Development.* RBI Speech at FICCI.
- Reserve Bank of India (2023). *Financial Stability Report.* RBI Publications.


### Deposit Insurance in India


- Deposit Insurance and Credit Guarantee Corporation (DICGC). (2022). *Annual Report.* DICGC, RBI.


### How RBI Monitors Banks: CRAR, NPA, etc.


- Reserve Bank of India (2022). *Report on Financial Stability in*

*India*. RBI.

- Mohan, R. (2006). *Monetary Policy and Exchange Rate Frameworks: The Indian Experience*. Reserve Bank of India Bulletin.

## NPA in the Indian Banking Sector

- Ranjan, R., & Dhal, S. C. (2003). *Non-Performing Loans and Terms of Credit of Public Sector Banks in India: An Empirical Assessment*. Reserve Bank of India Occasional Papers, 24(3), 81-121.
- Rajan, R. (2017). *I Do What I Do: On Reform, Rhetoric & Resolve*. HarperCollins India.

## Concept of Twin Balance Sheet Problem & Case Study in India

- Economic Survey of India (2017). *Chapter on Twin Balance Sheet Problem and Resolution Mechanism*. Ministry of Finance, Government of India.
- Sengupta, R., & Vardhan, H. (2019). *The Indian Banking Crisis: Resolution or Reformation?* Brookings India.

## Insolvency & Bankruptcy Concept, Measures in India

- Insolvency and Bankruptcy Board of India (IBBI). (2022). *Annual Report on Insolvency Resolution*. Government of India.
- Roy, S., & Sarkar, S. (2021). *Evaluating the Impact of the Insolvency and Bankruptcy Code in India*. Economic & Political Weekly, 56(7).

## Role of Asset Reconstruction Companies (ARCs) & ARCs in India

- Roy, A., & Prakash, S. (2022). *The Role of Asset Reconstruction*

*Companies in Indian Banking.* Indian Institute of Banking & Finance.

- Reserve Bank of India (2023). *Guidelines on Asset Reconstruction Companies.* RBI Notifications.

## Types of Banks and Non-Banking Financial Institutions (NBFIs)

- Reserve Bank of India. (n.d.). *Types of banks in India.*

### Non-Banking Financial Companies (NBFCs) in India

- Reserve Bank of India. (n.d.). *Frequently asked questions on Non-Banking Financial Companies (NBFCs).*

### NBFCs as Shadow Banks

- Policy Circle. (2022). *Shadow banks: NBFCs and their regulatory framework in India.*

### Chapter 5:
Difference Between Savings and Investment

- Investopedia. (2016). *Saving vs. Investing: Understanding the Key Differences.*

### Meaning of Market in Economics

- Investopedia. (2002). *Market: What It Means in Economics, Types, and Common Features.*

### Banking and Financial Market - The Two Pillars of the Financial System

- Corporate Finance Institute. (n.d.). *Financial Markets - Overview,*

*Types, and Functions.*

### Concept of Financial Market

Investopedia. (2006). *Financial Markets: Role in the Economy, Importance, Types, and Examples.*

### Types of Financial Market

- Corporate Finance Institute. (n.d.). *Financial Markets - Overview, Types, and Functions.*

### Capital Market and Everything Under This

- Investopedia. (2009). *Bond Market vs. Stock Market: What's the Difference?.*

### Difference Between Equity Market and Bond Market

- Investopedia. (2023). *Debt Market vs. Equity Market: What's the Difference?.*

### Primary and Secondary Markets Concept in Financial Market

- Investopedia. (2016). *Primary Market vs. Secondary Market: What's the Difference?.*

### Types of Bond/Debt Instruments

- Investopedia. (2012). *The Basics of Bonds.*

### Why Corporate Market Not So Developed in India

- Observer Research Foundation. (2023). *An Underdeveloped Corporate Bond Market: The Achilles' Heel of India's Growth Story.*

### Concept of Bond Yield

- Investopedia. (2012). *Bond Yield: What It Is, Why It Matters, and How It's Calculated.*

**Stock Market in India, Stock Exchanges in India**

- Investopedia. (2009). *Indian Stock Market: Exchanges and Indexes.*

**Difference Between Mutual Funds and Exchange Traded Funds**

- Charles Schwab. (n.d.). *ETFs vs. Mutual Funds – What's the Difference?.*

**Emergence of New Capital Instruments like REITs and InvITs in India**

- Bajaj Broking. (2024). *REITs and InvITs: Key Differences Explained for Investors.*

**Instruments of the Money Market and Role of the Money Market**

- Federal Reserve Bank of Richmond. (1998). *Instruments of the Money Market.*
- Corporate Finance Institute. (n.d.). *Money Market.*

**Concepts Under Derivative Market and Derivative Instruments**

- Investopedia. (n.d.). *Understanding Derivatives: A Comprehensive Guide to Their Uses and Risks.*
- Investopedia. (n.d.). *Derivatives 101: A Beginner's Guide.*

**Significance of Derivative Market**

- Investopedia. (n.d.). *Understanding Derivatives: A Comprehensive Guide to Their Uses and Risks.*

## Difference Between Hedging and Speculation

- Investopedia. (n.d.). *Hedging vs. Speculation: What's the Difference?.*
- Blueberry Markets. (n.d.). *Hedging vs Speculation: Top Differences.*

## Difference Between Forwards and Futures

- Investopedia. (n.d.). *Forward Contracts vs. Futures Contracts: What's the Difference?.*
- CME Group. (n.d.). *Futures Contracts Compared to Forwards.*

## Difference Between Futures and Options

- Investopedia. (n.d.). *Options vs. Futures: What's the Difference?.*

## Concept of Leverage in Financial Sector

- Investopedia. (n.d.). *Leverage Ratio: What It Is and How to Calculate.*
- Federal Reserve Board. (2024). *Leverage in the Financial Sector.*

## Concept of Leverage in Derivatives

- Investopedia. (n.d.). *Derivatives 101: A Beginner's Guide*

## What Are Credit Default Swaps

- Investopedia. (n.d.). *Credit Default Swap: What It Is and How It Works.*
- CFA Institute. (n.d.). *Credit Default Swaps.*

### The Whole Story of 2008 Global Financial Crisis


- Reserve Bank of Australia. (n.d.). *The Global Financial Crisis.*
- Federal Reserve History. (n.d.). *The Great Recession and Its Aftermath.*
- Wikipedia contributors. (n.d.). *2008 Financial Crisis.* Wikipedia, The Free Encyclopedia.


### What Are Bubbles in Financial Market


- Investopedia. (n.d.). *What Is an Economic Bubble and How Does It Work, With Examples.*
- Russell Investments. (n.d.). *Bursting The Myth: Understanding Market Bubbles.*


### Concept of Arbitrage


- Harvard Business School Online. (n.d.). *What Is Arbitrage? 3 Strategies to Know.*
- Investopedia. (n.d.). *What Is Arbitrage? Definition, Example, and Costs.*


### Chapter 6:
### Circular Flow of Income and Economic Sectors


- Central Statistics Office. (n.d.). *Gross Domestic Product: How it is Measured.*


### Injections and Leakages in the Economy


- Reserve Bank of Australia. (2018). *Injections and Leakages.*


### GDP Calculation Methods


- Central Statistics Office. (n.d.). *Gross Domestic Product: How it is Measured.*

### GDP Calculation in India

- Investopedia. (2024). *How Is the GDP of India Calculated?.*

### Multiplier Effect and Related Concepts

- Investopedia. (2024). *What Is the Multiplier Effect? Formula and Example.*
- Investopedia. (2024). *Marginal Propensity to Consume (MPC) in Economics, With Formula.*
- Investopedia. (2024). *Marginal Propensity to Save (MPS): Definition and Calculation.*

### Government Budget and Fiscal Concepts

- Investopedia. (2024). *Capital Expenditures vs. Revenue Expenditures.*
- Investopedia. (2024). *Fiscal Deficit: Definition and History in the U.S..*

### Freebies Culture and Subsidies in India

- Reuters. (2025). *India's top court says handouts creating 'class of parasites', Live Law reports.*

### Capital Expenditure and Disinvestment in India

- Investopedia. (2024). *Capital Expenditure (CapEx) Definition, Formula, and Examples.*

### Balanced Budget and Government Borrowings

- Investopedia. (2024). *Fiscal Deficit: Definition and History in the*

*U.S..*

### Virtuous and Vicious Cycles in the Economy

- Investopedia. (2024). *What Is the Multiplier Effect? Formula and Example.*

### Government Stimulus Packages and COVID-19 Responses

- Investopedia. (2024). *What Is the Multiplier Effect? Formula and Example.*

### Externalities and Environmental Impact

- Mankiw, N. G. (2020). *Principles of Economics* (9th ed.). Cengage Learning.
- Baumol, W. J., & Oates, W. E. (1988). *The Theory of Environmental Policy* (2nd ed.). Cambridge University Press.
- Hardin, G. (1968). The tragedy of the commons. *Science, 162*(3859), 1243-1248. https://doi.org/10.1126/science.162.3859.1243

### Negative Externalities & Climate Change

- Stern, N. (2006). *The Stern Review: The Economics of Climate Change.* HM Treasury.
- IPCC. (2021). *Climate Change 2021: The Physical Science Basis.* Cambridge University Press. https://www.ipcc.ch/ar6/wg1/
- Dasgupta, P. (2021). *The Economics of Biodiversity: The Dasgupta Review.* HM Treasury.

### Biomagnification as a Negative Externality

- Carson, R. (1962). *Silent Spring.* Houghton Mifflin.

## Urbanization and Environmental Degradation

- United Nations. (2019). *The World's Cities in 2018 – Data Booklet*. UN Department of Economic and Social Affairs.
- NASA. (2023). *Urbanization and Flash Floods: How Cities Affect Rainfall*.

## Climate Change and Least Developed Countries (LDCs)

- IPCC. (2022). *Climate Change 2022: Impacts, Adaptation and Vulnerability*. Cambridge University Press.
- UNFCCC. (2023). *Loss and Damage: Addressing the Harms of Climate Change*.

## Green Finance & Carbon Markets

- OECD. (2021). *Green Finance and Investment: Green Bonds Mobilizing Private Investment in Sustainable Infrastructure*.
- World Bank. (2023). *Carbon Markets: Overview and Recent Developments*.

## Economic Cycles and Recession

- Schumpeter, J. A. (1939). *Business Cycles: A Theoretical, Historical, and Statistical Analysis of the Capitalist Process*. McGraw-Hill.
- Minsky, H. P. (1986). *Stabilizing an Unstable Economy*. Yale University Press.
- National Bureau of Economic Research (NBER). (2023). *Definition of Recession and Business Cycles*.
- Reinhart, C. M., & Rogoff, K. S. (2009). *This Time is Different: Eight Centuries of Financial Folly*. Princeton University Press.

## 2008 Financial Crisis and Recession

- Krugman, P. (2009). *The Return of Depression Economics and the Crisis of 2008*. W.W. Norton & Company.
- Lewis, M. (2010). *The Big Short: Inside the Doomsday Machine*. W.W. Norton & Company.

### Yield Curve & Predicting Recession

- Federal Reserve Bank of St. Louis. (2023). *The Yield Curve and Recession Predictability*.
- Estrella, A., & Mishkin, F. S. (1996). *Predicting U.S. Recessions: Financial Variables as Leading Indicators*. The Review of Economics and Statistics, *80*(1), 45-61.

### Counter-Cyclical Fiscal Policy

- Keynes, J. M. (1936). *The General Theory of Employment, Interest, and Money*. Macmillan.
- Blanchard, O. (2020). *Fiscal Policy Under Low Interest Rates*. American Economic Association, *110*(4), 27-65.

### Behavioral Economics and Human Psychology in Finance

- Thaler, R. H. (2015). *Misbehaving: The Making of Behavioral Economics*. W.W. Norton & Company.
- Kahneman, D. (2011). *Thinking, Fast and Slow*. Farrar, Straus and Giroux.
- Tversky, A., & Kahneman, D. (1974). *Judgment under Uncertainty: Heuristics and Biases. Science*, *185*(4157), 1124-1131.

### Psychological Aspects of Economic Trends and Consumer Behavior

- Ariely, D. (2008). *Predictably Irrational: The Hidden Forces That Shape Our Decisions*. HarperCollins.

- Sunstein, C. R., & Thaler, R. H. (2008). *Nudge: Improving Decisions About Health, Wealth, and Happiness*. Yale University Press.

## AI Trends, Social Media & Consumption Psychology

- Netflix. (2020). *The Social Dilemma* [Documentary].
- Alter, A. (2017). *Irresistible: The Rise of Addictive Technology and the Business of Keeping Us Hooked*. Penguin Press.

## Hedonic Adaptation & Consumer Trends (Shopping Hauls, Unboxing, etc.)

- Brickman, P., & Campbell, D. T. (1971). *Hedonic Relativism and Planning the Good Society. Adaptation-Level Theory*, 287-305.
- Lyubomirsky, S. (2013). *The Myths of Happiness: What Should Make You Happy, but Doesn't, What Shouldn't Make You Happy, but Does*. Penguin.

## Social Media, Fast Fashion & Buy Now Pay Later (BNPL)

- McKinsey & Company. (2023). *Fast Fashion: Trends and Consumer Behavior*.
- World Economic Forum. (2022). *The Rise of Buy Now, Pay Later: A Behavioral Economic Perspective*.

## Psychology of Investment, 2008 Housing Crisis & Bank Runs

- Kindleberger, C. P., & Aliber, R. Z. (2005). *Manias, Panics, and Crashes: A History of Financial Crises* (5th ed.). Palgrave Macmillan.
- Akerlof, G. A., & Shiller, R. J. (2010). *Animal Spirits: How Human Psychology Drives the Economy, and Why It Matters for Global Capitalism*. Princeton University Press.
- Diamond, D. W., & Dybvig, P. H. (1983). *Bank Runs, Deposit*

*Insurance, and Liquidity. Journal of Political Economy, 91*(3), 401-419.

## Loss Aversion and Marketing Strategies

- Tversky, A., & Kahneman, D. (1991). *Loss Aversion in Riskless Choice: A Reference-Dependent Model. The Quarterly Journal of Economics, 106*(4), 1039-1061.